WE ALL COME IN DIFFERENT PACKAGES
Activities to Increase Handicap Awareness
Grades 3 - 6

Written by Dee Konczal and Loretta Pesetski
Illustrated by Beverly Armstrong
Edited by Sherri Butterfield

The Learning Works

The purchase of this book entitles the individual teacher to reproduce copies for use in the classroom.

The reproduction of any part for an entire school or school system or for commercial use is strictly prohibited.

No form of this work may be reproduced or transmitted or recorded without written permission from the publisher.

Copyright © 1983
THE LEARNING WORKS, INC.
P.O. Box 6187
Santa Barbara, CA 93160
All rights reserved.
Printed in the United States of America.

Introduction

We All Come in Different Packages is designed to make children more aware of handicaps and more understanding of people who have them. It contains individual and group activities to help children recognize the similarities and differences between themselves and people who are blind, communicatively handicapped, crippled, deaf, learning disabled, or retarded.

We All Come in Different Packages is divided into five sections.

- The **Introduction** acquaints children with the way handicaps may affect abilities, appearance, and feelings and gives them tips on how to relate more naturally to people who are handicapped.
- **Communicative Handicaps** covers aphasia, deafness, and disorders of articulation and fluency. It includes activities to make children aware of the ways sounds may be heard as distorted or muffled by people who are hard-of-hearing.
- **Physical Handicaps** covers visual impairment or blindness, certain bodily dysfunctions, and orthopedic handicaps. It includes activities to acquaint children with access symbols, the Braille alphabet, and the epileptic seizure sequence and posters to encourage sight saving and eye safety.
- **Learning Handicaps** covers disorders of attention, emotionality, memory, motor activity, perception, and symbolization. It includes mirror writing, riddles, visual perception activities, a word search, and the personal story of Colin Ruffner, a sixteen-year-old boy with a learning disability.
- **Mental Handicaps** mentions a variety of causes but deals with the one result: less-than-normal intellectual function, or retardation. It includes simulation activities, a word search, and the fictionalized story of Tom, a mentally retarded teen-ager.

Each section contains a brief introduction, bulletin board ideas, informative mini-posters, individual and group activity sheets, suggestions for additional correlated activities, topics for discussion, and a list of resources for extended study.

The activities in this book can be adapted easily to a wide range of age, grade, ability, and maturity levels. They may be used in any order as supplements to regular health and science units or as an independent adventure in affective education. An answer key is provided for those activities that are not open-ended.

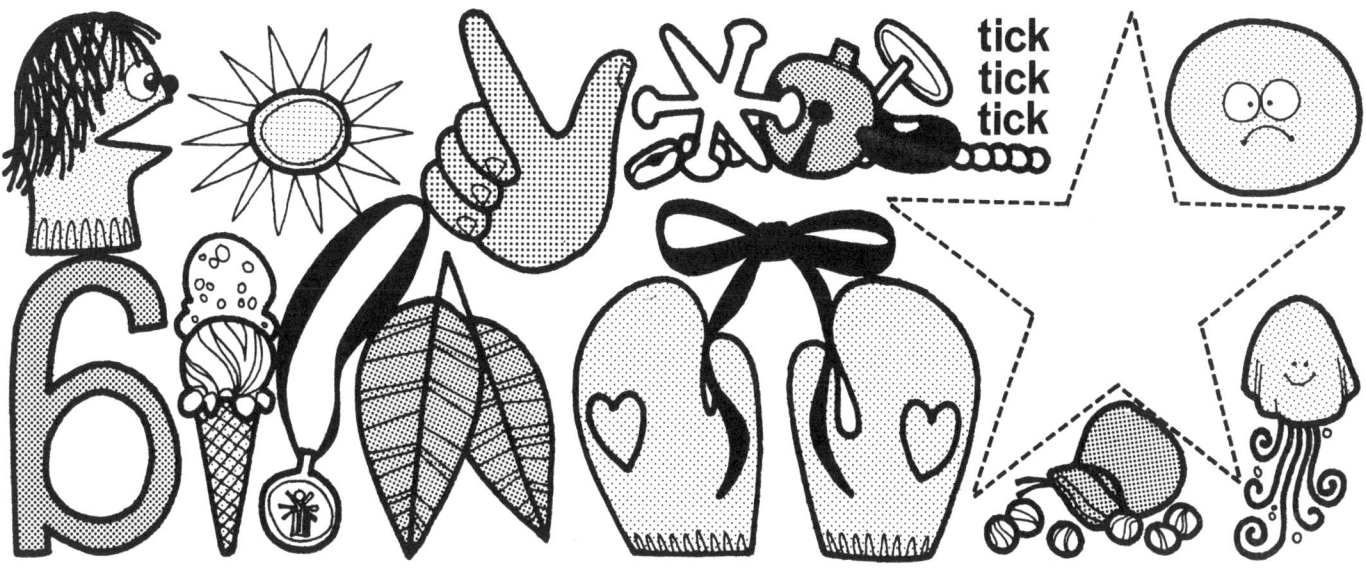

Contents

Introduction **6-19**
   Bulletin Board Idea . . . . We All Come in Different Packages 6
   Mini-Posters . . . . Mini-Posters 7-10
   Individual Activity Sheet . . . . Getting Your Head Together 11
   Individual Activity Sheet . . . . All People Have Feelings 12
   Individual Activity Sheet . . . . All People Have Talents and Handicaps 13
   Game . . . . Handicap Myth Game 14-17
   Group Activity Sheet . . . . Talking Sock Puppets 18-19

Communicative Handicaps **20-30**
   Introduction . . . . Communicative Handicaps 20
   Bulletin Board Idea . . . . Hear! Hear! 21
   Mini-Poster . . . . Decibels 22
   Mini-Poster . . . . A Friend Is Someone Who Communicates 23
   Mini-Poster . . . . Hearing Impairments 24
   Mini-Poster . . . . Hearing Aids 25
   Individual Activity Sheet . . . . Finger Spelling 26
   Group Activity Sheet . . . . Listen and Hear 27
   Group Activity Sheet . . . . Outspoken Speeches 28
   Additional Activity Ideas . . . . Correlated Activities 29
   Resource List . . . . Books and Films 30

Physical Handicaps **31-53**
   Introduction . . . . Physical Handicaps 31-32
   Bulletin Board Idea . . . . The Eyes Have It! 33
   Mini-Posters . . . . Sight-Saving Tips 34-37
   Individual Activity Sheet . . . . The Braille Alphabet 38
   Individual Activity Sheet . . . . Beastly Braille 39
   Group Activity Sheet . . . . Names in the News 40
   Group Activity Sheet . . . . Dots Do It 41
   Group Activity Sheet . . . . Spectacle Speculation 42
   Individual Activity Sheet . . . . Getting Acquainted with Little People 43-45
   Individual Activity Sheet . . . . Accessibility Survey 46-47
   Game . . . . Seizure Sequence Game 48-49
   Additional Activity Ideas . . . . Correlated Activities 50-51
   Resource List . . . . Books, Films, and Agencies 52-53

Learning Handicaps **54-69**
   Introduction . . . . Learning Handicaps 54
   Bulletin Board Idea . . . . Riddles, Riddles 55-56
   Mini-Posters . . . . Mini-Posters 57-58
   Individual Activity Sheet . . . . Fun with Words 59
   Individual Activity Sheet . . . . Can You Follow Directions? 60
   Individual Activity Sheet . . . . Following Directions 61
   Group Activity Sheet . . . . Aren't You Finished Yet? 62
   Individual Activity Sheet . . . . Aren't You Finished Yet? 63
   Group Activity Sheet . . . . Mirror Writing 64
   Individual Activity Sheet . . . . Double-Line Star 65

Contents
(continued)

Group Activity Sheet	Colin's Story	66-67
Additional Activity Ideas	Correlated Activities	68
Resource List	Books, Films, and Agencies	69

Mental Handicaps **70-83**

Introduction	Mental Handicaps	70
Bulletin Board Idea	Hello, I'm Retarded	71
Mini-Posters	Mini-Posters	72-74
Individual Activity Sheet	Fun with Words	75
Group Activity Sheet	Tom's Story	76
Individual Activity Sheet	Tom's Story	77-78
Group Activity Sheet	Smarties and Slowpokes	79
Individual Activity Sheet	Smarties and Slowpokes, Sheet I	80
Individual Activity Sheet	Smarties and Slowpokes, Sheet II	81
Additional Activity Ideas	Correlated Activities	82
Resource List	Books, Films, and Agencies	83

Glossary 84-85
Answer Key 86-87
Award 88

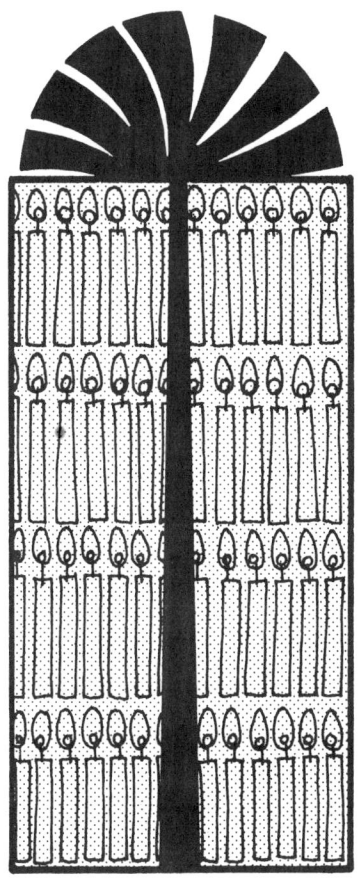

Introduction
Bulletin Board Idea

We All Come in Different Packages

Cover empty boxes with butcher, shelf, or wrapping paper in assorted bright colors. Use felt-tipped marking pens or paint to add facial features and other details. Decorate with buttons, fabric scraps, felt, paper, and ribbon. Add eyeglasses, hats, suspenders, and ties for a realistic touch. Stack the boxes against a wall or use tacks to attach them to a bulletin board. Add the message, **We All Come in Different Packages.**

We All Come In Different Packages
©1983—The Learning Works, Inc.

Mini-Posters

Put the mini-posters that follow on a bulletin board or use them in a learning center. Encourage children to design other posters on similar themes, and add them to the display.

Remember, we all have handicaps. Some are on the outside, and some are on the inside. Some are temporary, and some are permanent.

When you talk to a person with a hearing problem, stand in front and look directly at his or her eyes. Speak calmly and slowly. Form the words carefully so the person can read your lips, but don't exaggerate this motion.

Relax! If you don't know what to do or say, the person with the handicap will tell you.

Be a friend. Talk about things you both like. A person who has a handicap has many interests and hobbies just like you do.

Be alert to barriers that may be in your friend's way. Sometimes barriers cause more problems for a person with a handicap.

Introduction
Mini-Posters

Remember that a person with a handicap likes to eat your favorite food and go to your favorite places. He or she has feelings of love and hurt just like you do.

Help a handicapped person if you are asked or if the need is obvious, but don't insist if the person doesn't want to be helped.

Sometimes it takes a little longer for a person with a handicap to get things said or done. That's okay. Just wait and let the person set the pace.

Introduction
Mini-Posters

Don't be afraid to talk about the handicap.
Ask questions and listen carefully, but don't probe.
Be sensitive to the handicapped person's feelings.

Talk directly to the person
who has the handicap.
Don't ask someone else
when you can ask him or her.

Talk in a normal tone
to blind people.
You don't need to shout.
They can **hear** you
even though they cannot see.

Introduction
Individual Activity Sheet

Name _____

Getting Your Head Together

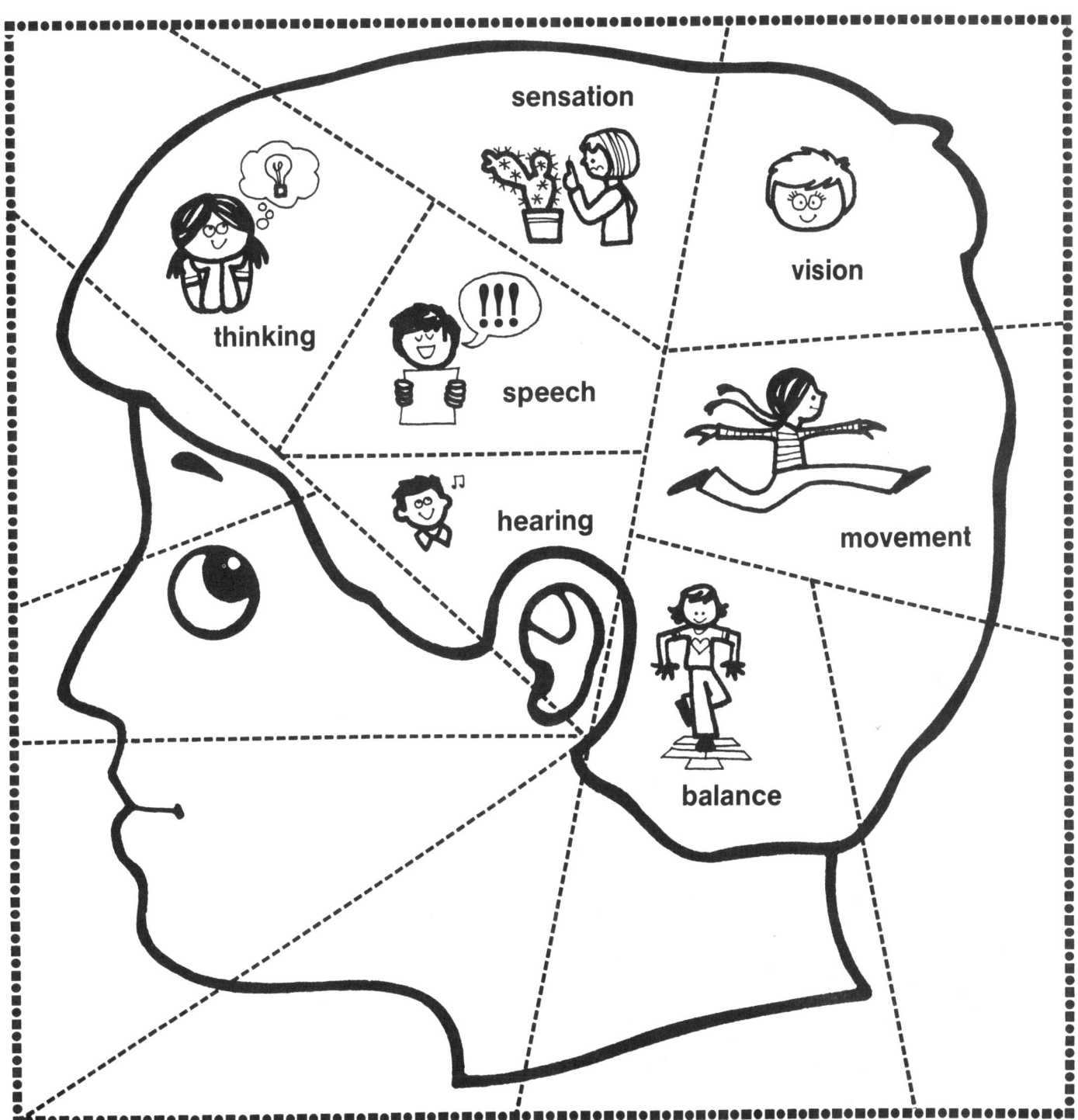

Each part of your brain helps your body do a different thing. Which parts will you use as you color this puzzle, cut the pieces apart, and put them back together again?

Sometimes when people are very sick or when their heads are hit very hard, parts of their brains are hurt. Then they may have trouble doing the things those parts helped them do—or they may not be able to do those things at all.

We All Come In Different Packages
©1983—The Learning Works, Inc.

Introduction
Individual Activity Sheet

Name _____

All People Have Feelings

People come in different packages. They look different. Some of them are tall, and some are short. Some of them are fat, and some are thin. They have different abilities. Some of them are strong and well coordinated while others are weak and find physical tasks difficult. Some are able to sing well, throw a ball hard, or work math problems fast, while others cannot do any of these things.

All people have feelings. They are sensitive about how they look and about what they can do. They may feel bad if they look different from other people or if they cannot do what others are able to do. They may be hurt when other people point out their inabilities or make fun of them because of their appearance.

What things are you sensitive about? Put a check mark in the box beside each thing you don't want people to make fun of or tease *you* about.

☐ my artificial limb	☐ my crooked spine	☐ my height
☐ my athletic ability	☐ my crossed eyes	☐ my knock-knees
☐ my big ears	☐ my crutches	☐ my laugh
☐ my big feet	☐ my deafness	☐ my musical ability
☐ my blindness	☐ my fingernails	☐ my nearsightedness
☐ my bowlegs	☐ my freckles	☐ my nose
☐ my braces	☐ my glasses	☐ my scar
☐ my cane	☐ my grades	☐ my shape
☐ my clothes	☐ my hair	☐ my speech
☐ my complexion	☐ my hands	☐ my teeth
☐ my coordination	☐ my hearing aid	☐ my voice

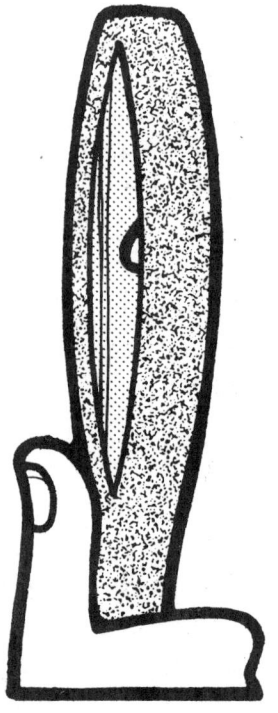

Introduction
Individual Activity Sheet

Name _____

All People Have Talents and Handicaps

Nobody can do everything well. Things that are easy for some people are very hard or even impossible for other people. Everyone is handicapped in some ways and talented in others. Indicate how well you can do each of these things by putting an **X** in one of the boxes beside it.

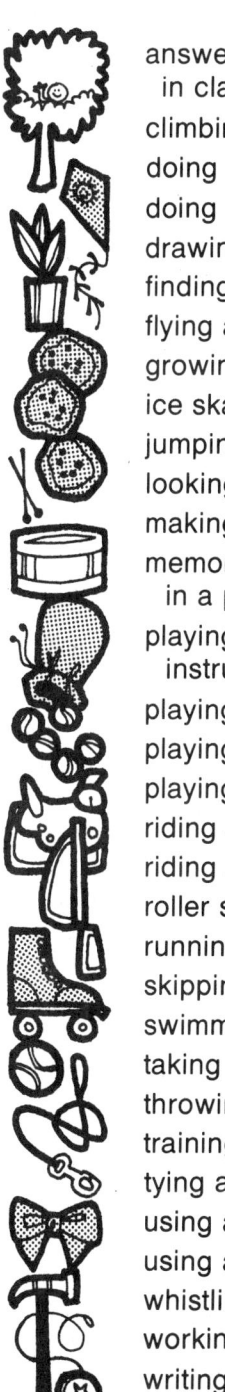

	For Me It's			I've Never Tried It
	Easy	**Hard**	**Impossible**	
answering a question in class				
climbing a tree				
doing long division				
doing a magic trick				
drawing a picture				
finding something out				
flying a kite				
growing a plant				
ice skating				
jumping rope				
looking something up				
making cookies				
memorizing a part in a play				
playing a musical instrument				
playing chess				
playing marbles				
playing soccer				
riding a bicycle				
riding a horse				
roller skating				
running fast				
skipping				
swimming				
taking a test				
throwing a ball				
training a dog				
tying a bow				
using a hammer				
using a sewing machine				
whistling				
working a yo-yo				
writing a story				

We All Come In Different Packages
©1983—The Learning Works, Inc.

Introduction
Game

Handicap Myth Game

This game may be played by small groups or by the entire class.

To prepare the myth cards, duplicate pages 14-17. Cut along the solid lines, fold along the broken lines so that the words are on the outside, and then staple.

To play the game, deal an equal number of cards to each one of the players. Direct the players to read both sides of the cards, decide which side is the fact, and then lay their cards down in front of them with the facts up. Discuss the facts and myths. In this game, as in life, the winners are those who can distinguish one from the other.

1A
You cannot always tell if people are handicapped by looking at them.

1B
You can always tell if people are handicapped by looking at them.

2A
A child with a hearing aid hears everything in the same way as a child with normal hearing.

2B
A child with a hearing aid does not hear everything in the same way as a child with normal hearing.

3A
A child with a severe hearing loss can learn to speak.

3B
A child with a severe hearing loss cannot learn to speak.

4A
Blind people can get around by themselves.

4B
Blind people cannot get around by themselves.

5A
Mentally retarded people don't know or care when you make fun of them.

5B
Mentally retarded people have feelings and can be hurt like everyone else.

6A
Not all deaf people can read lips.

6B
All deaf people can read lips.

We All Come In Different Packages
©1983—The Learning Works, Inc.

Handicap Myth Game
(continued)

7A People with cerebral palsy are mentally retarded.	**7B** People with cerebral palsy may be very intelligent.
8A Many mentally retarded children look just like other children.	**8B** All mentally retarded children look different from other children.
9A People who are legally blind have no useful vision.	**9B** People who are legally blind may be able to see many things.
10A Every handicap has only one cause.	**10B** Many handicaps have more than one cause.
11A Cerebral palsy is a condition, not a contagious disease.	**11B** Cerebral palsy is a contagious disease.
12A Blind people have an extra sense that helps them detect obstacles and find their way around.	**12B** Blind people do not have an extra sense but may learn to use their senses of sound and touch and their memories to get around.
13A Not all handicapped people are mentally retarded.	**13B** All handicapped people are mentally retarded.
14A Children with Down's syndrome are always happy and easygoing.	**14B** Children with Down's syndrome are sometimes sad and angry.

Handicap Myth Game
(continued)

15A People with visual handicaps need help in everyday living.	**15B** People with visual handicaps can live and work independently.	**16A** It is okay to pet or play with a guide dog when it is working.	**16B** You should not pet or play with a guide dog when it is working.
17A Handicapped children always misbehave.	**17B** Like other children, handicapped children sometimes misbehave.	**18A** Closed captions make it possible for deaf people to enjoy television.	**18B** Closed captions are a useless nuisance and make it hard for people with normal hearing to enjoy television.
19A With concentration and practice, visually handicapped children can learn to rely on their other senses.	**19B** Visually handicapped children automatically develop their other senses.	**20A** Mentally retarded people cannot learn.	**20B** Mentally retarded people can learn.
21A Most children with learning disabilities could do better if they worked harder.	**21B** Many children with learning disabilities are working as hard as they can.	**22A** Blind people find it easy to eat foods that are served in large pieces and portions.	**22B** Blind people find it easier to eat foods that are served in small pieces and bite-sized chunks.

Handicap Myth Game
(continued)

23A Blind children don't like to watch television.	**23B** Blind children do like to watch television.
24A Children with learning disabilities don't want friends and don't like to play.	**24B** Children with learning disabilities want to have friends and like to play.
25A Children with learning disabilities can learn to read.	**25B** Children with learning disabilities cannot learn to read.
26A Children with speech problems may be smart.	**26B** Children with speech problems are stupid.
27A People with epilepsy are mentally ill.	**27B** People with epilepsy are not mentally ill.
28A Using your eyes does not weaken your vision.	**28B** If people with visual handicaps use their eyes too much, their sight will get worse.
29A The best way to communicate with deaf people is to say the same thing over and over until they understand.	**29B** The best way to communicate with deaf people may be to write your message.
30A Children with learning disabilities are stupid.	**30B** Children with learning disabilities may be smart.

Introduction
Group Activity Sheet

Talking Sock Puppets

Purpose
This activity enables children to experience many kinds of handicaps firsthand.

What You Need
The materials listed below are for one child making one puppet. If many children are involved, you will need to increase the quantities and measurements accordingly. If you do not have enough of the handicapping devices (that is, the blindfolds, gloves, and eyeglasses) for each child, do this activity with small groups and have children take turns.

- old eyeglasses
- clear nail polish
- Q-tips
- handkerchief or scarf to use as a blindfold
- sock
- pantyhose for stuffing
- glove
- rubber band
- tagboard cut in a three-inch circle
- tacky glue
- felt scraps for facial features
- wig or yarn for hair
- scissors

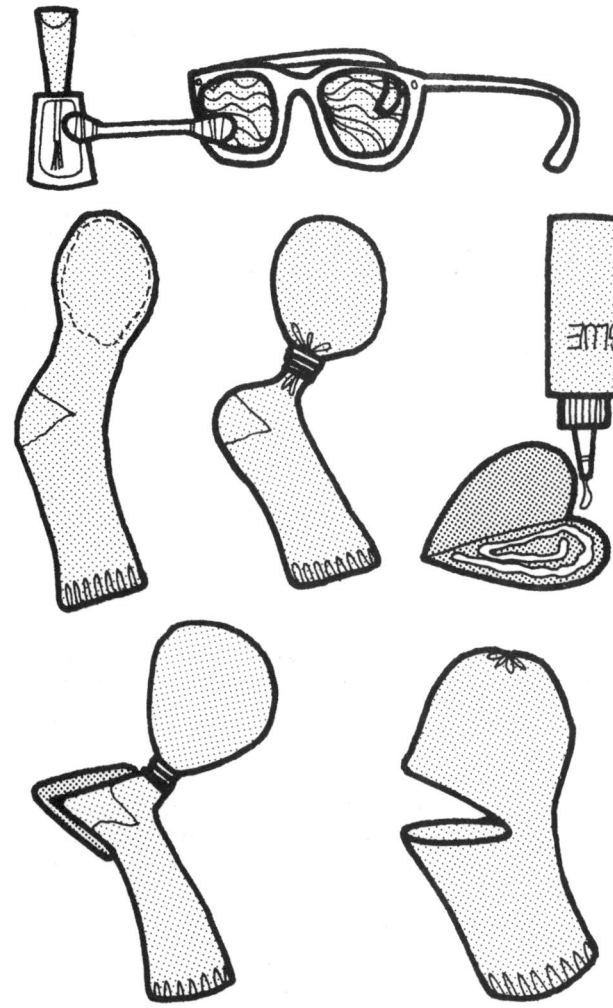

What You Do

1. Paint the eyeglass lenses with clear nail polish.
2. Use Q-tips to put "squiggles" in the polish before it dries.
3. Put a blindfold over your eyes.
4. Turn the sock wrong side out.
5. Stuff the sock with pantyhose from the toe halfway to the heel.
6. Take off the blindfold and put on the glove.
7. Put the rubber band around the sock to hold the stuffing in. Twist it several times to make it really tight.
8. Take off the glove.

(Mouth Directions 9 and 10 to the children so that they have to lip-read.)

9. Crease the tagboard circle in the middle.
10. Put glue all over one side of the circle. This circle will be the puppet's mouth.
11. Put on a pair of squiggly glasses.
12. Put the tagboard mouth over the widest part of the sock heel. Hold it for five minutes until the glue dries.
13. Turn the sock right side out.
14. Take off the glasses and put one hand in your pocket or under the table.

Introduction
Group Activity Sheet

Talking Sock Puppets
(continued)

15. Cut eyes, nose, and lips from felt.
16. Cut hair from the wig or the yarn.
17. Take your hand out of your pocket.
18. Glue the facial features and the hair to the puppet.
19. Let the glue dry.

Related Activities

- Talk about making the puppet. Was doing so harder than usual for most of the children? Why?
- Talk with the children about how their temporary handicaps made them feel. Did they feel awkward, frustrated, or angry when tasks that are usually simple became difficult?
- Use finished puppets to express feelings, represent handicapped children, or role play situations involving handicapped people.

We All Come In Different Packages
©1983—The Learning Works, Inc.

Communicative Handicaps

Communication determines the kinds of relationships we have and what happens to us in the world. The way we communicate tells other people about us and how we feel about ourselves. The child with a communicative handicap has trouble learning to communicate and may have problems acquiring social skills. Because language is basic to all learning, children who have communicative handicaps may also have difficulty learning academic skills. They may have trouble learning to order their world with language.

Children with communicative handicaps include those who are deaf, hard-of-hearing, or aphasic, or who have disorders of fluency or articulation.

The deaf are unable to hear and understand speech even with a hearing aid. The hard-of-hearing have hearing losses that are sufficient to interfere with normal communication even with the use of a hearing aid. Three of every one hundred school children have hearing impairments.

Aphasic children, or those with severe language handicaps, are children who have not developed language in the normal way. They have normal intelligence, but have difficulty learning to express themselves and to understand others.

Communication may also be affected by disorders of fluency, such as stuttering, which is an interruption in the rhythm of speech. Stuttering is characterized by hesitations, repetitions, or prolongations of sounds, syllables, words, or phrases. About one-half million children in the United States stutter.

Articulation disorders are difficulties with the way sounds are formed. These disorders account for about three-fifths of all communicative problems.

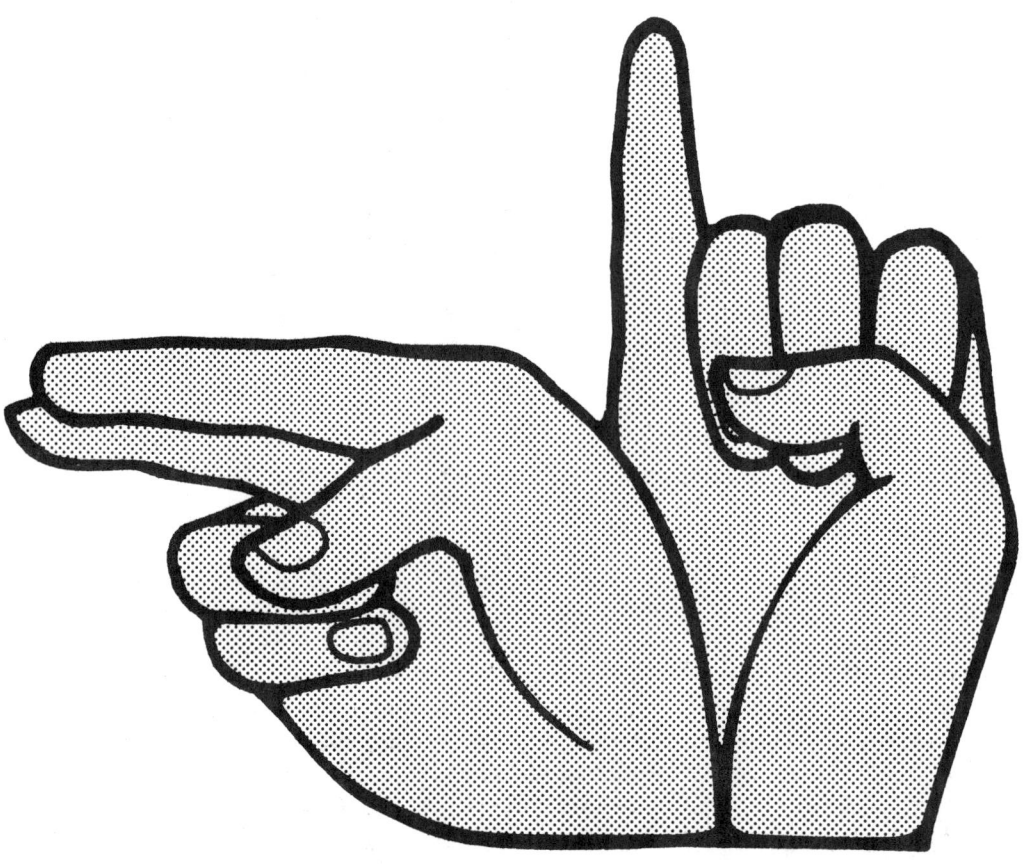

Communicative Handicaps
Bulletin Board Idea

Hear! Hear!

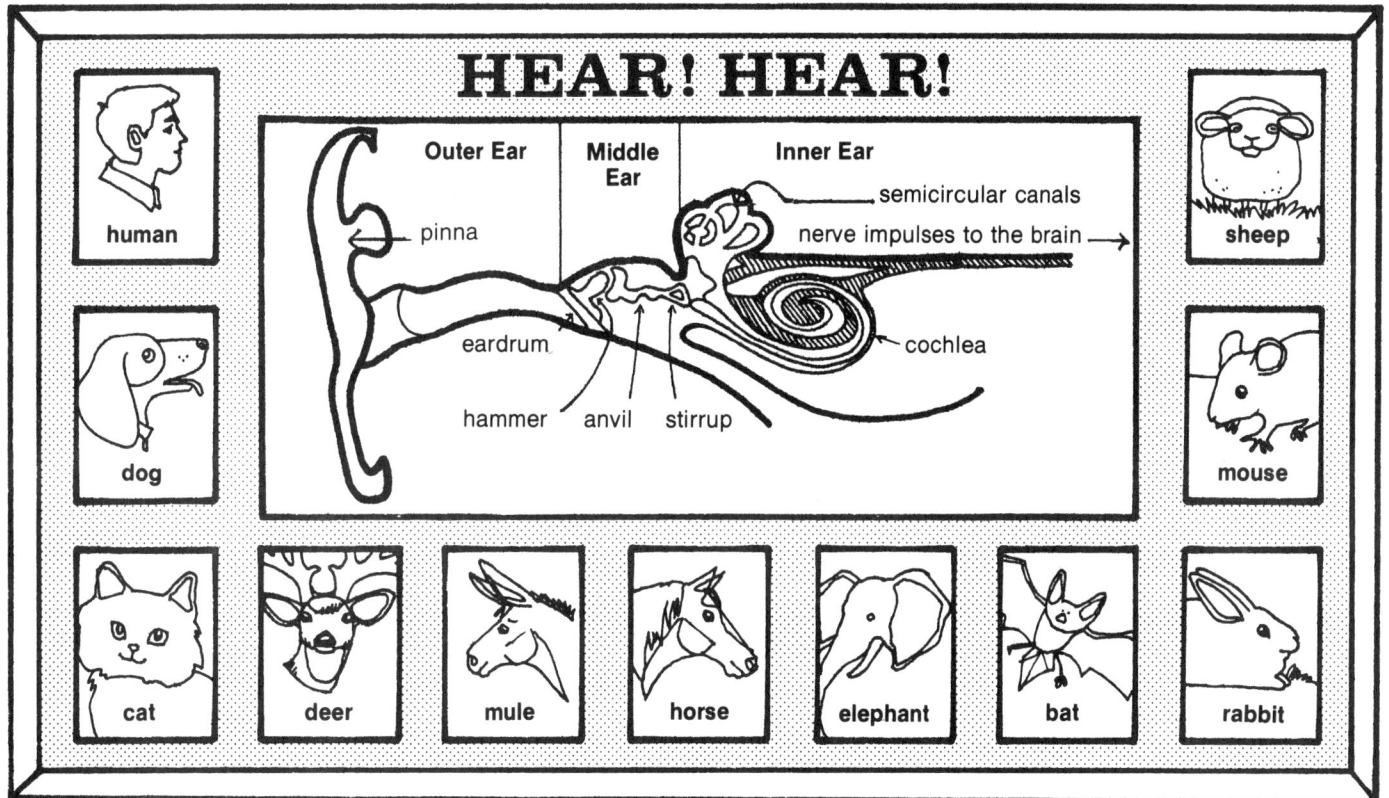

What You Need

- paper letters to spell **Hear! Hear!**
- a labeled anatomical drawing of the human ear
- drawings or photographs of a variety of ears, including some belonging to people and some belonging to animals

What You Do

1. Put the words **Hear! Hear!** at the top of the bulletin board.
2. In the center of the board, post the anatomical drawing.
3. Arrange a variety of ear pictures around the drawing.
4. Encourage students to add pictures and drawings to the display.

Related Activities

- Use the anatomical drawing as the basis for a simple explanation of how the ear works. Talk about the divisions of the ear, its parts, and their functions. Ask such questions as, *In what form does sound travel? What purpose does the pinna serve? Where do sound waves enter the ear? How are they amplified? What part of the ear is sensitive to their vibrations?*
- Use the other drawings and photographs as the basis for a discussion of the similarities and differences between ears. Ask such questions as, *Do you think most elephants hear well? Why? Would you expect a rabbit to hear better than a person? Why or why not?*
- Talk about famous people, such as Ludwig van Beethoven and Helen Keller, who have been hard-of-hearing or deaf. List their names on the chalkboard and discuss their individual accomplishments.

Decibels

Noise can be measured. Noise is measured in units called **decibels**. The greater the number of decibels, the louder the noise. Most of the sounds you hear measure between 30 and 80 decibels. If you listen to sounds louder than 85 decibels for a long time, they may harm your hearing.

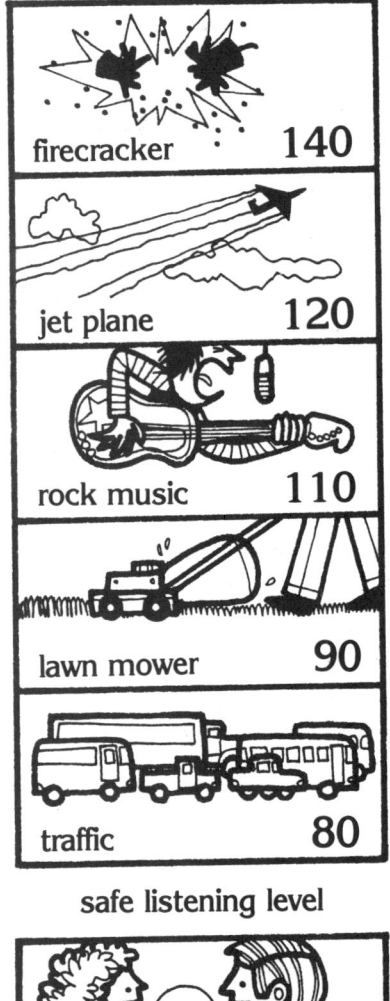

firecracker	140
jet plane	120
rock music	110
lawn mower	90
traffic	80

safe listening level

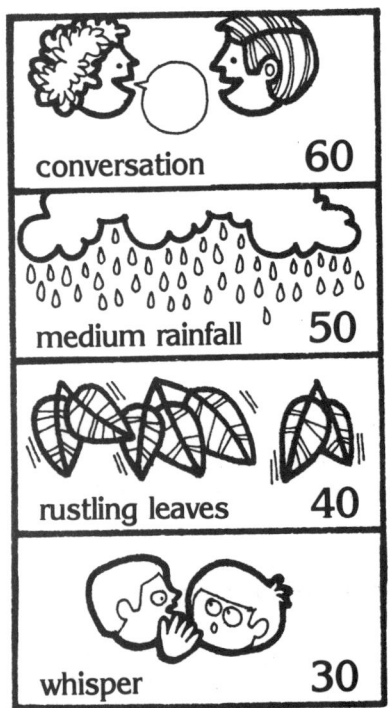

conversation	60
medium rainfall	50
rustling leaves	40
whisper	30

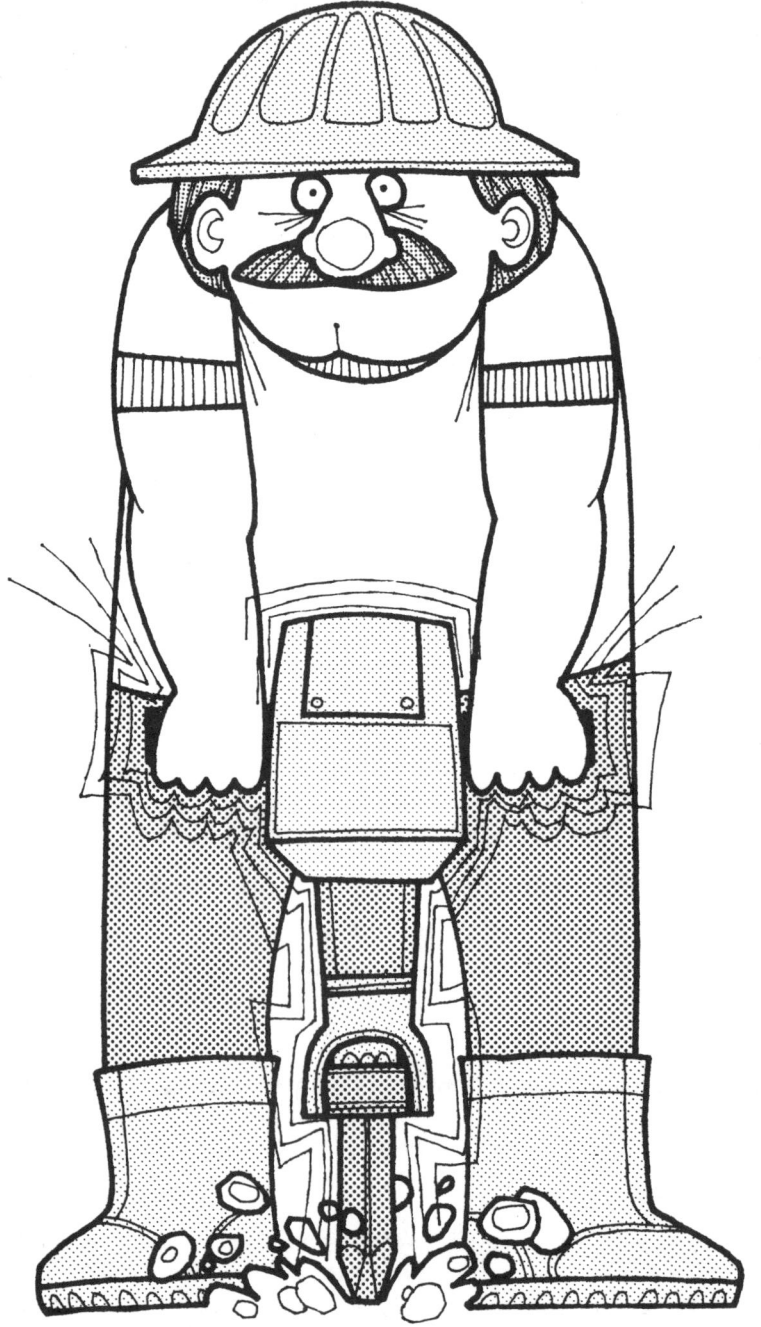

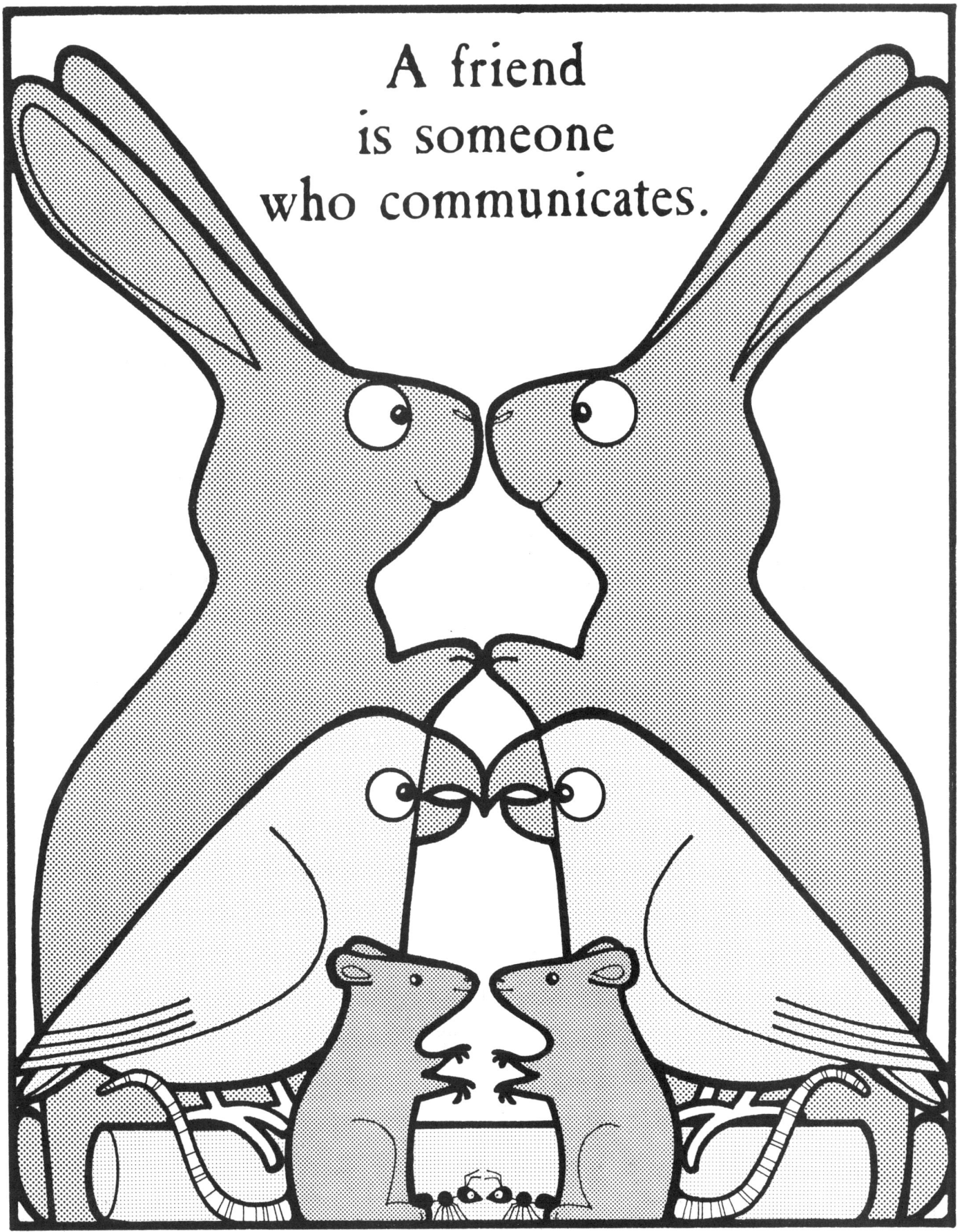

Hearing Impairments

Hearing impairments affect **3** of every **100** school children.

Hearing impairments may be **caused** by
- the aging process
- birth defects
- certain drugs
- earwax
- head injuries
- heredity
- middle ear infections
- prolonged or repeated exposure to loud noise
- tumors
- viral infections

Some hearing impairments can be **prevented** by
- avoiding loud noises whenever possible
- having your hearing tested periodically
- not putting anything smaller than your elbow into your ear
- seeing a doctor when your ear hurts
- wearing hearing protectors when you must work or play near loud noise
- wearing protective headgear when there is some danger that your head may be bumped, hit, or knocked while you work or play

Hearing Aids

Many people with hearing impairments can benefit from using hearing aids. Hearing aids amplify sounds, or make them louder and easier to hear. There are several kinds of hearing aids. Some of them are worn on the body, and some are worn in or near the ear. All of them are powered by batteries and have tiny microphones to collect sounds. They have switches so that the wearer can control the loudness, or volume, of the sound he or she hears.

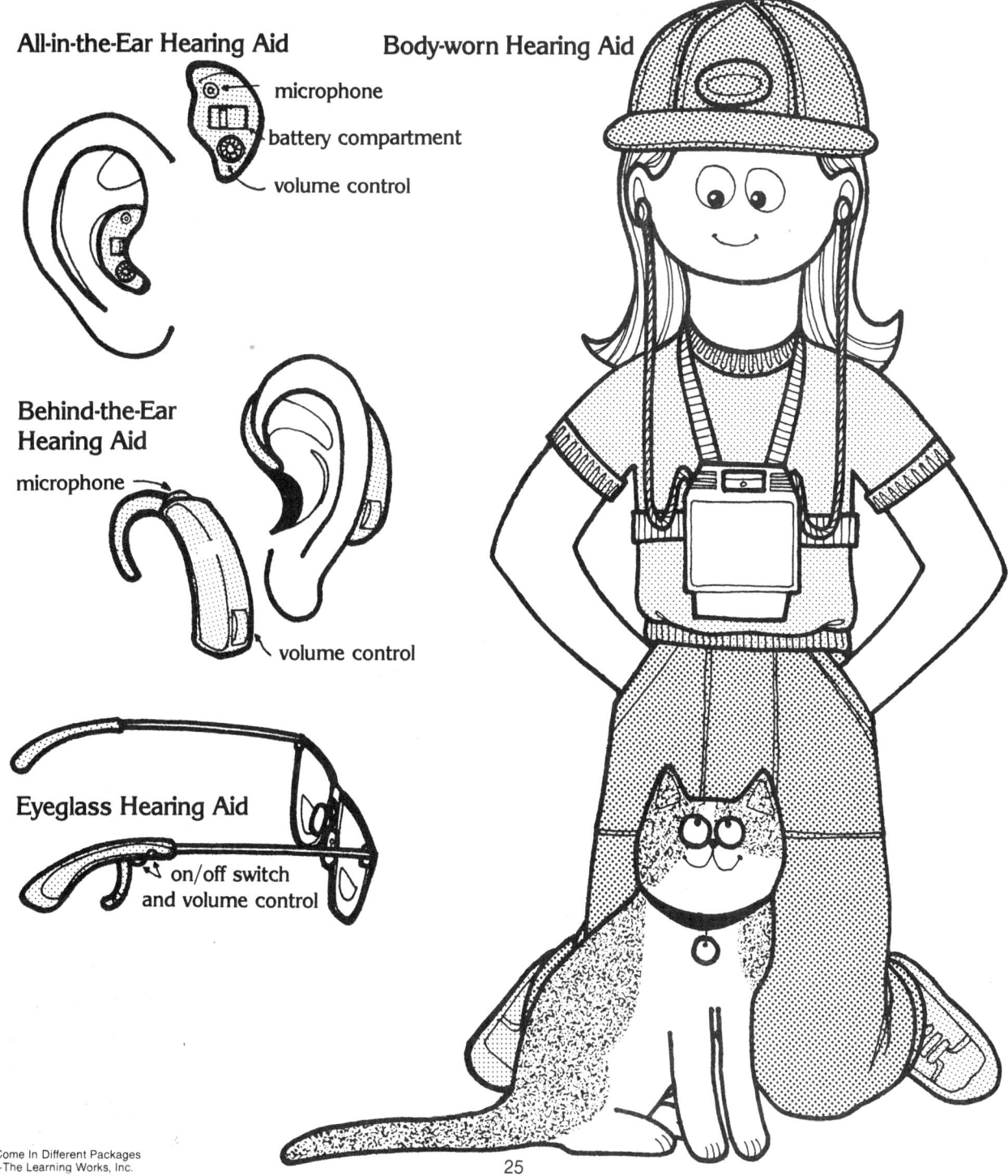

Communicative Handicaps
Individual Activity Sheet

Name _____

Finger Spelling

Some people who cannot hear learn to spell and speak with their fingers. The alphabet for finger spelling is pictured below. Use it to practice finger spelling your name, a greeting, and a word that names a feeling.

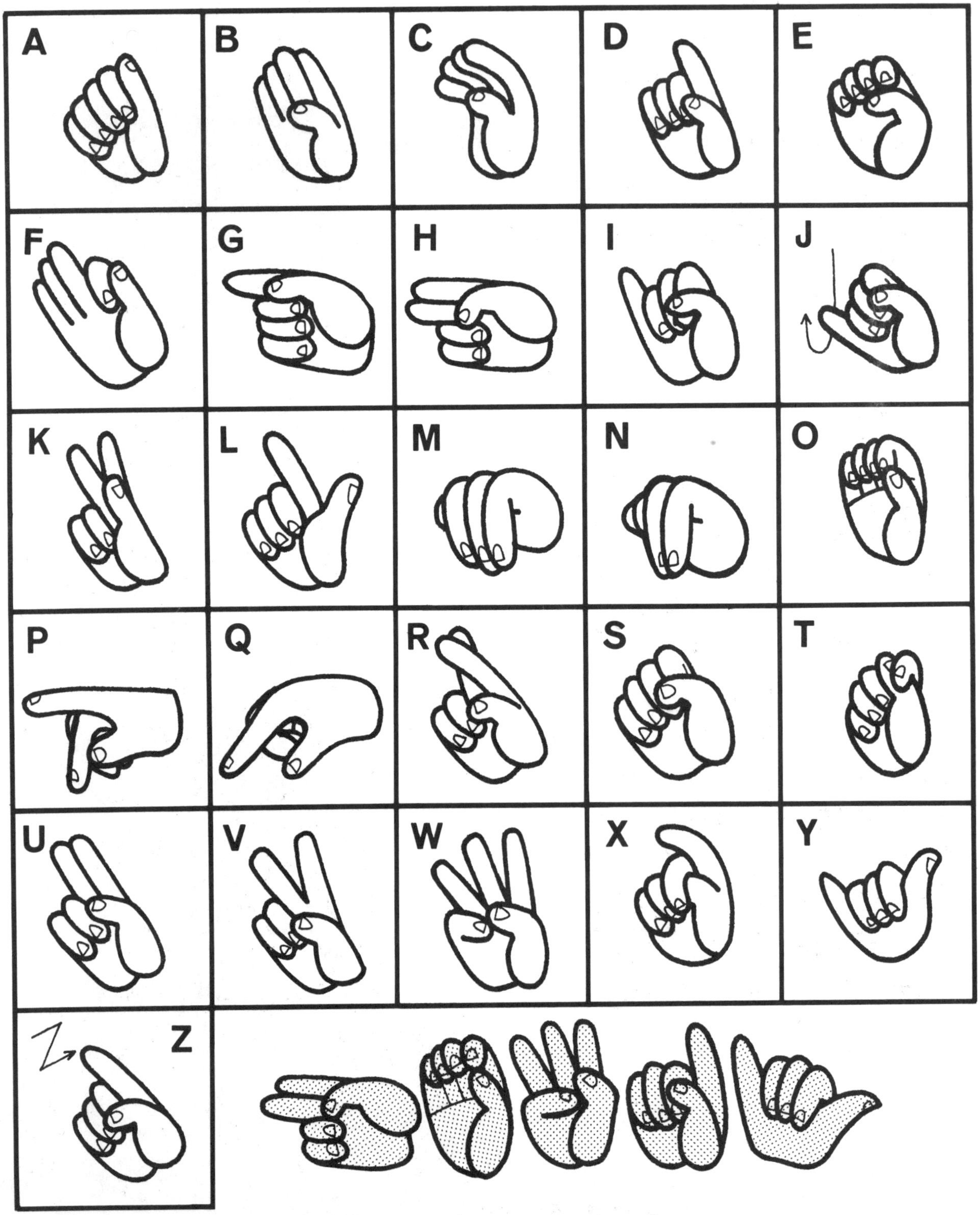

We All Come In Different Packages
©1983—The Learning Works, Inc.

Communicative Handicaps
Group Activity Sheet

Listen and Hear

Purpose

This activity helps children become aware of the ways in which a hearing loss interferes with communication and may affect academic learning.

What You Do

1. Read the following paragraph in a normal voice.

    There are many types of educational programs for hearing-impaired children. Some hearing-impaired children need help from resource teachers and/or speech and language specialists. Many things affect a hearing-impaired child's ability to do well in school. Among them are the degree and type of loss and the child's intelligence and motivation.

2. Have the students put their hands over their ears. Then read the paragraph again. Talk about how the sound is muffled. (A conductive hearing loss is common in school age children.)

3. Read the paragraph again with your hand or a handkerchief over your mouth. Again, talk about how the sound is muffled, or made softer, and changed, or distorted. (A sensorineural hearing loss means a child hears at a lower level and with distortion.)

4. Have the class listen to a radio station whose signal is weak and characterized by static. (Improperly fitted or damaged hearing aids may emit static like this.)

5. Discuss some of the difficulties involved in communicating with a hearing loss.

Communicative Handicaps
Group Activity Sheet

Outspoken Speeches

Purpose

This activity helps children become aware of the frustrations faced by their classmates who need to work with a speech or language specialist.

What You Do

1. Read the following examples to the class, one at a time.
2. After you read an example, discuss both the listener's and the speaker's feelings during communication. Emphasize the speaker's frustrations.

Average Speaker

A speech disorder is not funny. It can be very embarrassing to the speaker. Even a mild disorder can cause a misunderstanding.

Articulation Disorder

A thpeech dithoda ith not funny. It can be vewy embawathing to the thpeaka. Even a mild dithoda can cauthe a mithunduthtanding.

Stuttering

A-a-a-a ssspeech d-d-d-isorder is not f-f-funny. It c-c-can be, uhm, you know, uhm very embaaaarrassing to the the-the speaker. Eeeven a m-mild dis-dis-disorder can cause a *(cough)* mis-mis-mis-misunderstanding.

Language Disorder

No say words right. Can't. Not funny. Talk; feel hurt, sad.

Communicative Handicaps
Additional Activity Ideas

Correlated Activities

1. Have your students create a montage with pictures of ears in the center surrounded by pictures of things ears can hear. Discuss with your students the sounds that the pictures represent. Ask students to duplicate some of the sounds.

2. Initiate a class discussion of deafness. Then have your students write about what they would not be able to hear if they were deaf. What sounds would they miss the most? What problems would they have?

3. Educational supply companies have environmental sounds on cassette tapes. Obtain and play an environmental sounds tape. Have children match these sounds with the pictures or photos that accompany the tape or with the pictures on their montage.

4. Fill pairs of film canisters, plastic margarine tubs, or plastic Easter eggs with measured amounts of objects such as dried beans or peas, cornmeal or sand, and paper clips. Tape the filled containers shut with masking, electrician's, or duct tape. Invite children to shake the containers and pair the ones that sound the same. Then suggest that they try to identify the contents of each container by sound alone.

Books and Films

Books for Children

Baker, Margaret Joyce. *The Sand Bird.* Nashville, Tenn.: Thomas Nelson, 1973. Upper elementary.

Charlip, Remy, and Mary Beth. *Handtalk: An ABC of Finger Spelling and Sign Language.* New York: Parents Magazine Press, 1974. Primary.

DeGering, Etta. *Gallaudet, Friend of the Deaf.* New York: David McKay, 1964. Upper elementary and junior high.

Glazzard, Margaret H. *Meet Camille and Danille: Hearing Impaired.* Lawrence, Kans.: H & H Enterprises, 1978. Primary.

Green, Constance M. *The Unmaking of Rabbit.* New York: Viking, 1972. Upper elementary and junior high.

Henry, Marguerite. *King of the Wind.* Chicago, Ill.: Rand McNally, 1948. Upper elementary and junior high.

Hunter, Edith F. *Child of the Silent Night: The Story of Laura Bridgman.* Boston, Mass.: Houghton Mifflin, 1963.

Johnson, Ann Donegan. *The Value of Giving: The Story of Beethoven.* La Jolla, Calif.: Value Communications, 1979. Elementary.

_____ . *The Value of Determination: The Story of Helen Keller.* La Jolla, Calif.: Value Communications, 1976. Elementary.

Johnston, Catherine D. *I Hear the Day.* South Waterford, Maine: Merriam-Eddy, 1977.

Lee, Mildred. *The Skating Rink.* Boston, Mass.: Houghton Mifflin, 1969. Upper elementary and junior high.

Levine, Edna. *Lisa and Her Soundless World.* New York: Human Sciences Press, 1974. Elementary.

Litchfield, Ada B. *A Button in Her Ear.* Niles, Ill.: Albert Whitman, 1976. Elementary.

Martin, Patricia Miles. *Thomas Alva Edison.* New York: G. P. Putnam's Sons, 1971. Elementary.

Peter, Diana. *Claire and Emma.* New York: Harper & Row – John Day Junior Books, 1977. Primary.

Peterson, Jeanne W. *I Have a Sister, My Sister is Deaf.* New York: Harper & Row, 1977. Primary.

Robinson, Veronica. *David in Silence.* New York: Harper & Row, 1965. Upper elementary and junior high.

Spence, Eleanor. *The Nothing Place.* New York: Harper & Row, 1965. Upper elementary and junior high.

Young, Percy Marshall. *Beethoven.* Port Washington, N.Y.: David White, 1966. Elementary.

Films and Filmstrips

Can You Hear Me? Free on request from 3M Company Film Lending Service, 220-6W, 2501 Hudson Road, St. Paul, Minnesota, 55119.

Gordon. From the Feeling Free Film Series by Scholastic Services.

Hello, Everybody. Filmstrip series available from SFA, Box 851, Pasadena, California, 91102.

Kids Come in Special Flavors Classroom Kit from the Kids Come in Special Flavors Company, Box 562, Forest Park Station, Dayton, Ohio, 45405.

Life Line to the World of Sound. Free on request from Modern Talking Pictures, 1212 Avenue of the Americas, New York, New York, 10036. 13 minutes.

My New Friend. Eyegate.

Why Am I Different? Barr Films.

Physical Handicaps

Children with physical handicaps include those who are visually handicapped, those who are orthopedically handicapped, and those who have a disorder of body function.

Visual Impairment

There are degrees of visual impairment. People who are **partially sighted** usually have a visual acuity between 20/70 and 20/200 *after* the best possible correction has been obtained. This means that they see at a distance of twenty feet what a person with unimpaired vision sees at a distance of seventy to two hundred feet. People who are **legally blind** have less than 20/200 acuity after correction; however, they can see. They are readily able to distinguish light from dark and may also be able to read large print. People who are **totally blind** often can distinguish light from dark and see large forms.

A youngster may be born with a visual impairment or acquire a visual disability through injury or disease. Visually impaired youngsters can do almost everything other youngsters can do. At home or in a familiar environment, they do not need help to find their way around. They rely on memory and on the sense of touch. When they are older and travel, they may use a cane, a partner, or a guide dog to help them.

Orthopedic Handicap

An orthopedic handicap is a crippling condition that interferes with the normal function of bones, joints, or muscles. This category includes such widely disparate conditions as missing limbs, cerebral palsy, and spina bifida.

Children may be born with orthopedic handicaps such as club feet, missing limbs, and spina bifida. After birth, they may acquire orthopedic disabilities such as deformed limbs, immobility, or muscle weakness. The causes for these problems may be heredity, toxic agents taken by the mother, birth injuries, accidents, infections, and diseases such as juvenile arthritis, muscular dystrophy, osteomyelitis, and poliomyelitis.

Cerebral palsy refers to a group of conditions caused by damage to the motor centers of the brain. It is sometimes the result of an inadequate supply of oxygen to the brain before, during, or immediately after birth, but may be caused by other factors as well.

There are three main types of cerebral palsy. The child who is **spastic** has jerky, uncontrolled movements. The child who is **athetoid** has uncontrollable movements. The child who is **ataxic** is awkward and has trouble with balance. In addition to motor dysfunction, children with cerebral palsy may have learning difficulties, psychological problems, sensory defects, mental retardation, and convulsive disorders. The school-age child with cerebral palsy is treated both for cerebral palsy and for the associated disorders.

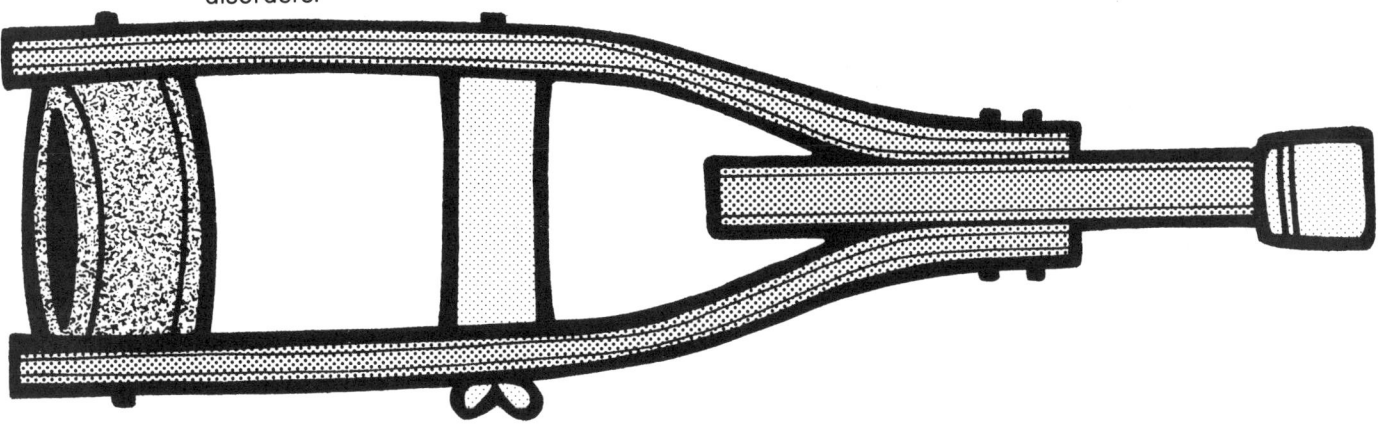

Physical Handicaps
(continued)

Spina bifida is the number one birth defect in the United States. It affects one in every thousand newborns, or eight thousand of the babies born in this nation each year. When children have this defect, one or more of their spinal vertebrae fail to close completely. The spinal cord and nerves bulge through the resultant opening and form a sac filled with fluid and covered with a fragile membrane. The relatively unprotected nerves within this sac can be easily injured, and the risk of paralysis and infection is high. The current treatment for spina bifida is to close the opening surgically within twenty-four hours after birth. Depending on the size of the opening and the amount of nerve damage, children with spina bifida may ride in wheelchairs, use crutches, or walk unassisted.

More than 75 percent of the children who have spina bifida also have hydrocephalus, a condition in which fluid builds up within the skull and causes pressure on the brain. Doctors can relieve this condition by inserting a thin plastic tube in the brain and shunting away the excess fluid.

Disorders of Body Function

Disorders of body function, such as asthma, diabetes, and severe allergies, may set limits on a child's activities that are as frustrating as those created by visual or orthopedic handicaps. A diabetic child may need to eat measured amounts of food at prescribed intervals and to take medication regularly. An asthmatic child may not be able to tolerate prolonged periods of vigorous activity that would tax the respiratory system. Children with severe allergies may have to be cautioned about exposure to allergens and watched for the symptoms that signal the onset of a severe or life-threatening reaction requiring immediate treatment.

Physical Handicaps
Bulletin Board Idea

The Eyes Have It!

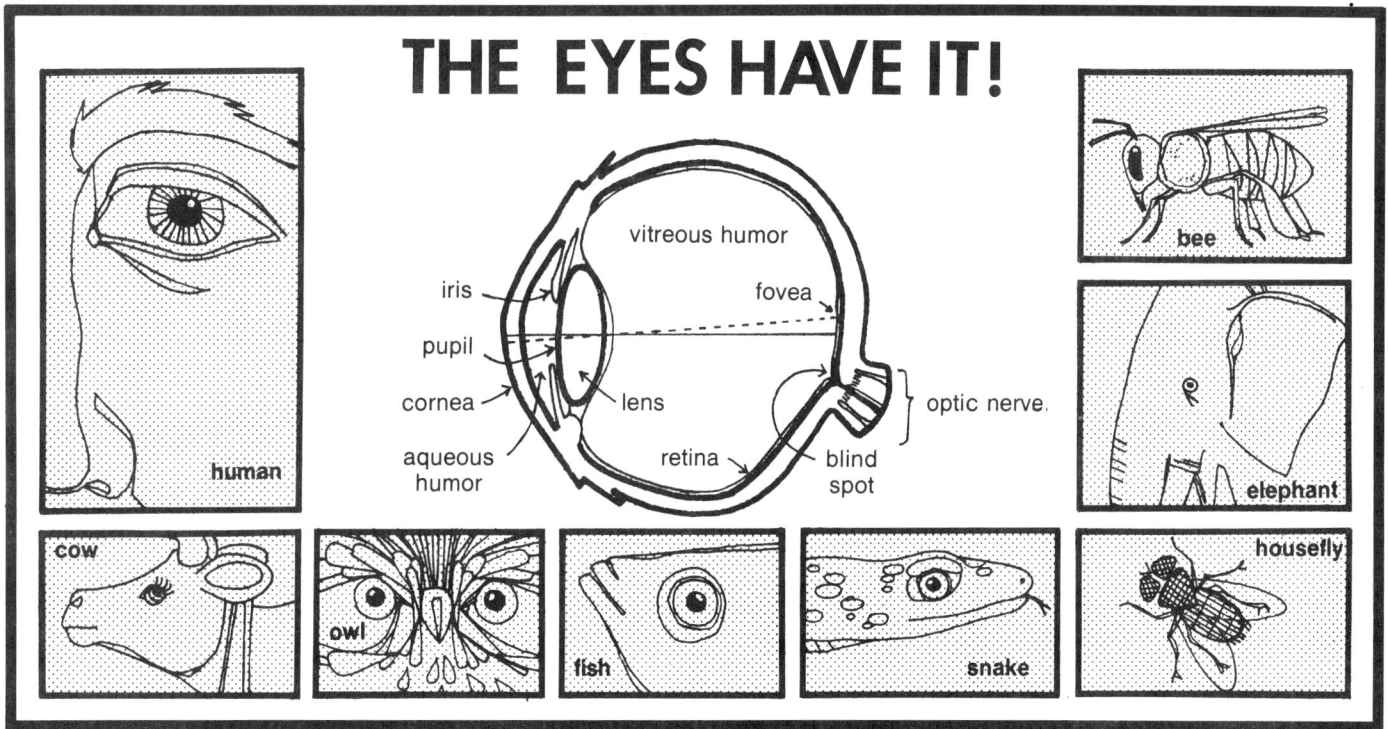

What You Need
- paper letters to spell **The Eyes Have It!**
- a labeled anatomical drawing of the human eye
- drawings and photographs of a variety of eyes, including some belonging to people and some belonging to animals and insects

What You Do
1. Put the words **The Eyes Have It!** at the top of the bulletin board.
2. In the center of the board, post the anatomical drawing.
3. Arrange a variety of eye pictures around the drawing.
4. Encourage students to add pictures and drawings to the display.

Related Activities
- Vision is the richest and most stimulating of our senses. Two-thirds of our information about the outside world comes to us through our eyes. Use the anatomical drawing as the basis for a discussion of the parts of the eye and how it works. Ask, *In what ways does the eye resemble a camera? In what ways does the eye differ from a camera? How does the eye focus an image on the retina? What determines the focal length of the eye? How might illness or injury make the eye unable to see?*
- Louis Braille was a French organist and teacher of the blind who devised a system of raised-point writing for literature and music. This system makes it possible for sightless people to read with their fingertips. Have interested class members do some research to find out more about Louis Braille. How and at what age did he become blind?
- Write to the Communication Center, State Services for the Blind, 1745 University Avenue, St. Paul, Minnesota, 55104, for a free copy of the special alphabet Louis Braille devised. Send a self-addressed, stamped envelope and request a Braille alphabet sheet. Challenge interested students to see how many Braille letters they can learn to recognize by touch alone.

Physical Handicaps
Mini-Posters

Sight-Saving Tips

Sight-Saving Tips

Use sharp or pointed objects with care.
Always keep them away from your face.

When you get something in your eye, don't rub it.
Ask an adult for help.

Sight-Saving Tips

Never look directly at the sun.

Always avoid glare.

Wear safety glasses when you work with tools or near flying particles.

Physical Handicaps
Individual Activity Sheet

Name _____

The Braille Alphabet

Louis Braille was a French organist and teacher of the blind. He developed a system of raised-dot writing for literature and music. This remarkable system, called the Braille alphabet, makes it possible for people who cannot see to read with their fingertips.

The Braille alphabet is based on a rectangle made up of six dot positions. By changing the number of dots used and varying their positions within the rectangle, Louis Braille was able to come up with enough variations to represent twenty-six letters, ten numerals, and all needed punctuation marks.

Within the rectangle, each dot position has a number. Different combinations of these positions represent different letters, numerals, and punctuation marks, and even indicate when a letter should be capitalized. For example, a dot in position 1 represents the letter **a**. A combination of dots in positions 2, 5, and 6 stands for a period. A dot in position 6 *before* a letter indicates that the letter should be capitalized.

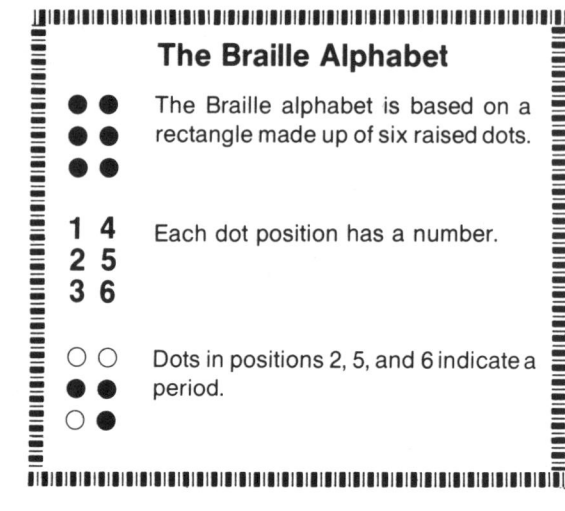

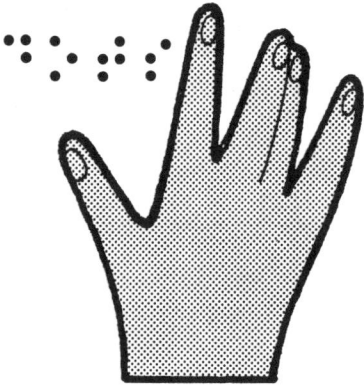

Braille Alphabet Chart

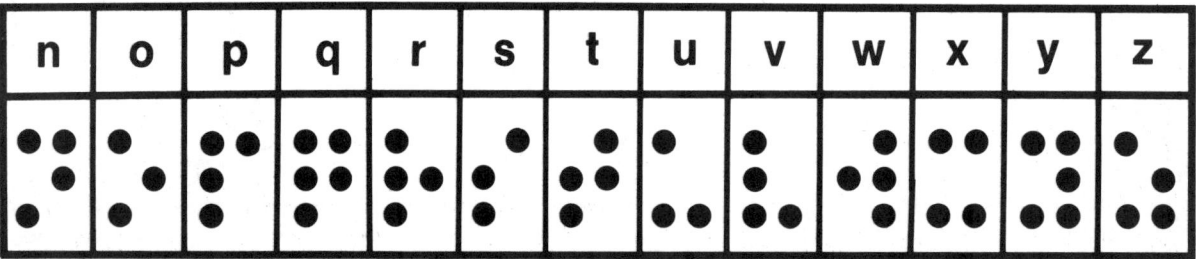

Physical Handicaps
Individual Activity Sheet

Name _____

Beastly Braille

In the Braille system, each dot position has a number. Each letter can be described by the sequence of numbers that name the positions of the dots used to represent that letter. For example, the letter **c** could be called 1-4, and the letter **z** could be called 1-3-5-6. Use the chart on page 38 to answer the following questions.

1. What number sequence would you use to describe the letter **b**? _____
2. What number would you use to describe the letter **a**? _____
3. What number sequence would you use to describe the letter **t**? _____
4. What series of number sequences would you use to write the word **bat**?

_____   _____   _____

5. Use Braille dots to write the word **bat** in the boxes on the right.

6. Use Braille dots to write the words **guinea pig** in the boxes on the right.

7. Use Braille dots to write the word **jellyfish** in the boxes on the right.

8. Use Braille dots to write the name of some animal in the boxes below. Then exchange papers with a friend and see if he or she can identify your beast and write its name in letters.

We All Come In Different Packages
©1983—The Learning Works, Inc.

Physical Handicaps
Group Activity Sheet

Names in the News

Purpose

The twofold purpose of this activity is to acquaint children with the Braille alphabet and to make them more aware of newsmakers and current events.

What You Need

- twenty-five sequentially numbered three-by-five index cards with a name written in Braille on each one. (Names should be taken from the newspaper and might include national leaders, political figures, show business personalities, sports heroes, and the like. Cut off the upper right-hand corner of each card so children can tell top from bottom.)
- additional blank index cards
- a bowl, box, or hat to hold the name cards
- a bowl, box, or hat to hold the fact cards
- enough copies of the Braille alphabet from page 38 for each child to have one
- paper
- pencils

What Students Do

Number your paper from one through twenty-five.

2. One at a time, take name cards from the container.
3. Identify the letters written in Braille on the card.
4. Note the number on the card, and print the name on your paper beside that number.
5. When you have identified all of the names, select one name and find out more about the person to whom it belongs. Where was this person born? In what country does this person live? What did he or she do that was newsworthy?
6. For bonus points, write one fact about this person in Braille on one side of a blank index card.
7. Key this fact card to the correct name card by writing the name card number on the other side of the fact card.
8. Put the fact card in the fact card container.

Related Activities

- As students read the names written in Braille and print them in letters on their papers, tell them to identify the persons to whom these names belong by office, title, or achievement.
- When the number of fact cards has grown sufficiently large, challenge students to match name cards with fact cards and to check the accuracy of their matches by comparing the numbers on the fronts of the name cards with those written on the backs of the fact cards.

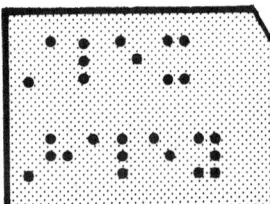 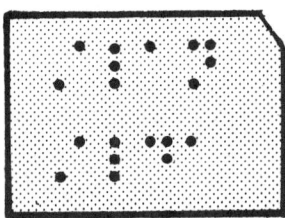 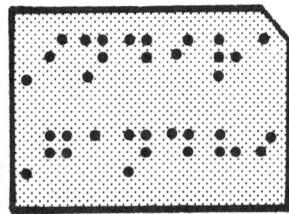

We All Come In Different Packages
©1983—The Learning Works, Inc.

Physical Handicaps
Group Activity Sheet

Dots Do It

Purpose
This activity helps children become better acquainted with the Braille alphabet and lets them practice working in pairs.

What You Need
- enough copies of the Braille alphabet from page 38 for each child to have one
- paper
- pencils

What Students Do
1. Choose a partner.
2. Write a message to your partner in Braille. As you write, leave plenty of space between the lines. Don't forget to indicate capital letters and to use periods when they are needed.
3. Check the Braille letters you have written against the alphabet on page 38 to be certain that the dots are in the correct places.
4. When you are certain that the Braille message you have written is correct, give it to your partner.
5. Ask your partner to read your message, transcribe it in the space you have left, and write a reply in Braille on a separate sheet of paper for you to transcribe.

Related Activities
- Suggest that students who are interested and have become proficient in Braille write their spelling or vocabulary words in it.
- Invite a blind or sighted person who reads Braille to visit your class and read a story from a Braille book. Ask the guest to demonstrate how to track, explain Grade I and Grade II Braille, show how to read music written in Braille, and/or demonstrate computer Braille.
- Obviously having *sighted* children work with dots they can *see* is not the same as having *sightless* persons work with dots they can only *feel*. If possible, do the activity on page 40 or this page with materials actually written in raised dots. The State Department of Education, Clearinghouse-Depository for the Visually Handicapped, 721 Capitol Mall, Sacramento, California, 95814, maintains a listing of volunteer transcriber groups in California. The Department of Rehabilitation maintains a list of braillists who may be asked to prepare materials for classroom use.

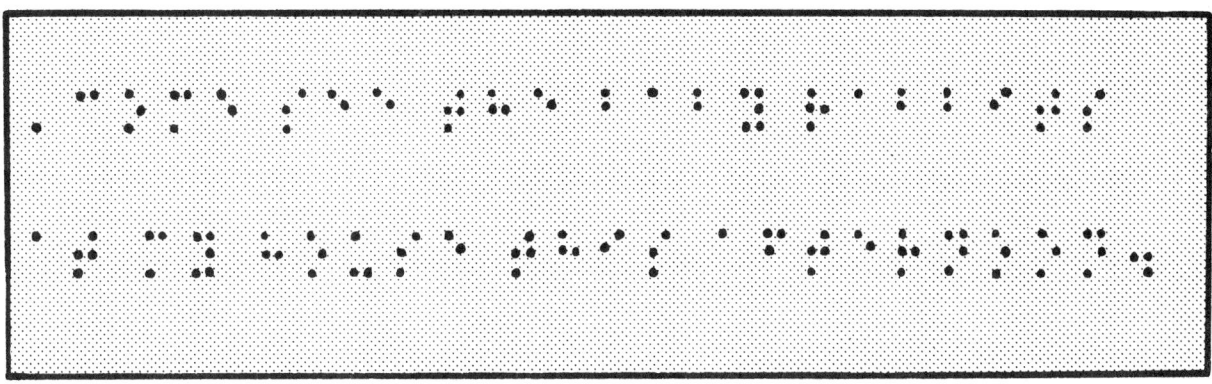

Physical Handicaps
Group Activity Sheet

Spectacle Speculation

Purpose

This activity helps children who have never worn eyeglasses or had problems with their vision to understand and empathize with those who wear spectacles and/or must work despite visual handicaps.

What You Need

- a copy of the book *Spectacles* by Ellen Raskin (New York: Atheneum, 1972)
- a mirror
- eyeglass frames without lenses (Obtain discarded frames from an oculist, optician, or optometrist, or ask students to bring some from home.)
- squiggled glasses prepared for the activity described on page 18

What You Do

1. Read the book to the class.

2. Talk about Laurel's need for eyeglasses.

3. Make the mirror and eyeglass frames available on a desk or table, or at a learning center.

4. Suggest that children take turns trying on frames and looking at themselves in the mirror.

5. Talk with children about how it feels to wear glasses.

6. Have students simulate monocular, tunnel, or blurred vision by (1) putting a paper patch over one eye, (2) putting paper patches with single holes punched in them over both eyes, or (3) wearing squiggled glasses.

7. Challenge students to do an assignment while their vision is artificially impaired in one of these ways.

8. Talk with students about how these experiences made them *feel.* On the basis of their feelings, encourage them to speculate about how it feels to be *permanently* visually handicapped and to wear glasses *all* of the time.

Related Activities

- Ask a student who has a vision problem and wears glasses to talk with the class about some of his or her experiences.
- If possible, obtain a copy of the Snellen chart and explain how it is used to test visual acuity.
- If convenient, arrange for the school nurse or some other qualified person to do vision screening in your classroom while students watch and ask questions.

Physical Handicaps
Individual Activity Sheet

Name _____

Getting Acquainted with Little People

Being very small or very large can be a physical handicap because so many of the things we wear and use are made for people who are of average size. People who are unusually small or unusually large often have trouble buying clothes, cars, and furniture. Nothing really seems to fit.

Being very small or short is a hereditary condition. It is not a disease. It is not contagious. A small person may have parents of average size. Small parents may have children of average size.

People who are very small or short are called **little people**. There are two kinds of little people. A **midget** has normal proportions but is short. A **dwarf** has a regular-sized body but short arms and legs. In this way, a midget is like a chihuahua—a small dog—and a dwarf is like a basset—a dog with an average sized body but very short legs.

We All Come In Different Packages
©1983—The Learning Works, Inc.

Physical Handicaps
Individual Activity Sheet

Name _____

Getting Acquainted with Little People
(continued)

Many little people are fewer than 48 inches tall when fully grown, and some of them are as short as 24 inches.

How tall are you? _____ inches

How tall is your mom? _____ inches

How tall is your dad? _____ inches

Kneel but remain upright. Do not sit back on your heels. Ask a friend to measure you.

How tall are you in this position? _____ inches.

Many little people are this same size.

What does it feel like to be a little person? Go through your house on your knees.

Can you reach light switches and faucets? _____

Can you see things on countertops and tables? _____

Try this same activity at school. On the lines below, list six things you can usually reach in your classroom but could not reach if you were a little person.

_____   _____

_____   _____

_____   _____

Getting Acquainted with Little People
(continued)

When you see a little person having trouble reaching or doing something, offer to help, but do not insist on helping. Little people like to be independent whenever they can be.

Most little people do not think of themselves as being handicapped because there are so many things that they can do. With special hand controls, a little person can drive a regular car.

Little people have been big entertainers. They have played important roles on stage, in motion pictures, and on television. Billy Barty has appeared on the stage and screen for many years. The Munchkins in *The Wizard of Oz* were played by little people, as were the Oompa-Loompas in *Willy Wonka and the Chocolate Factory*. A little person in a special costume created the walking version of E.T. in Steven Spielberg's movie.

Little people can be architects, authors, engineers, and musicians. They can be photographers, scientists and teachers—or almost anything. In fact, this book was illustrated by a dwarf.

Accessibility Survey

In the past, curbs, stairs, narrow doors and hallways, and other similar barriers have made rooms and buildings inaccessible to some people who were physically handicapped. Handicapped people in wheelchairs could not go to or move about in these places. Recently, the government has passed laws to eliminate barriers in public areas. Rooms and buildings that are accessible to the handicapped have been marked with a simple drawing of a person in a wheelchair. This drawing is called an **access symbol**.

Survey your school for accessibility. After you have checked and measured the facilities, place an **X** in the appropriate column.

Yes	No

1. Are there handicapped children or adults in your school?

2. Are extra-wide parking spaces reserved for the handicapped and marked with the access symbol?

3. Can doors and floors be reached by using ramps and elevators rather than only by climbing stairs?

4. Are all doors at least 32 inches wide?

5. Can exterior building and interior classroom doors be swung wide with a single push or pull?

6. Are halls and walkways at least 48 inches wide?

7. Are all light switches no more than 48 inches from the floor?

8. Can someone in a wheelchair use the bathroom?

9. Are sinks 29 to 34 inches from the floor?

Physical Handicaps
Individual Activity Sheet

Name _____

Accessibility Survey
(continued)

	Yes	No
10		
11		
12		

10. Do the faucets have lever-type controls?

11. Can someone in a wheelchair use the drinking fountain?

12. Is the access symbol posted in some places at your school? If so, list these places on the lines below.

_____   _____

_____   _____

_____   _____

13. Briefly describe some of the barriers you noticed while you were making your accessibility survey.

_____

_____

_____

14. Choose one of these barriers and tell how it could be eliminated or removed so that your school would be more accessible.

_____

_____

_____

15. According to your survey, how would you rate your school?

☐ completely accessible   ☐ mostly accessible   ☐ mostly inaccessible   ☐ completely inaccessible

Seizure Sequence Game

Children observing an epileptic seizure will be less frightened if they are aware that the epileptic's behavior follows a predictable pattern, or sequence, and if they are familiar with this pattern so that they know what to expect.

Photocopy the instruction card on this page and the picture cards on page 49. Make several copies so that more than one child can play the game at a time. Cut out the instruction card. Cut the picture cards apart. To make them more durable, glue them to tagboard or to plain three-by-five-inch index cards. For self-checking, number all of the cards in order on the back. To keep the card sets separate, use a different color to number the picture cards in each six-card set. Laminate the cards or cover them with clear Contact paper.

Talk with class members about **epilepsy**. Be certain they understand that it is a condition, *not* a contagious disease. Explain that a person who has epilepsy is called an **epileptic**. Describe the behavior sequence that characterizes most epileptic **seizures**. Tell the children what you will do if a class member has a seizure and how they can help you.

Make the sets of one instruction card and six picture cards available at a game table or learning center. Encourage class members to use the cards during their free time to review what has been said about the seizure sequence.

Seizure Sequence Game

1. Spread out all six picture cards.
2. Read the words and look at the pictures.
3. Recall the seizure sequence we discussed in class.
4. Arrange the cards in the order in which the pictured events can be expected to happen.
5. Check your arrangement by looking at the numbers on the backs of the cards.

Physical Handicaps
Game

Seizure Sequence Game
(continued)

Some of the cells in an epileptic's brain act up, causing him to lose control of his body for a short time.

The epileptic falls down.

People nearby should clear the area of anything that might hurt the epileptic.

The epileptic goes into convulsions. He may shiver or shake, make strange noises, roll his eyes, foam at the mouth, wet his pants, or do other unusual things. He cannot hear or speak. He does not realize what he is doing.

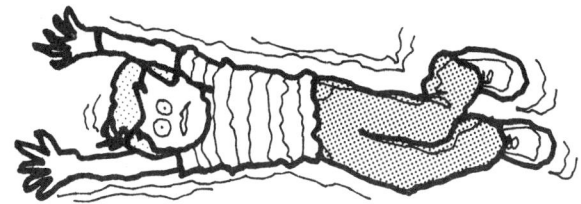

The epileptic feels tired and may want to rest. He probably does not remember what happened.

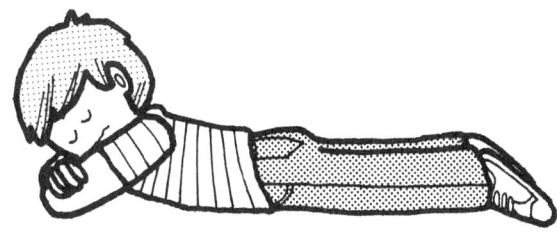

The epileptic will behave normally again. He will smile and run and play.

Physical Handicaps
Additional Activity Ideas

Correlated Activities

1. To make students aware of how it feels to have trouble with fine motor control, have them wear mittens, socks, or rubber gloves on their hands while they write, do math, untie and tie their shoes, button or zip their jackets, or play a game like marbles or jacks. Later, encourage students to write or tell about their experiences and discuss their feelings.

2. To make children more aware of how inaccessible some places are to people in wheelchairs, have them make montages depicting barriers to the handicapped or draw posters advocating accessibility.

3. Suggest that each student choose a physical handicap and write a brief essay in which he describes the handicap and tells how his home and school would have to be modified for his safety, comfort, and convenience if he had that handicap.

4. For a creative writing assignment, suggest titles that relate to physical handicaps. For example, you might use some of the following:

     The Wild Wheelchair Ride
     A Brace for Casey
     Sperry's Spectacular Spectacles
     My Two-Wheeler Is a Chair
     I Can't Do Much with a Crutch

5. Set up an obstacle course using chairs, desks, traffic cones, tires, rocks, logs or boards, and a ramp. Borrow wheelchairs from local rental agencies, hospitals, or special schools. Have students who are *not* physically handicapped attempt to negotiate the course in the chairs. Afterward, encourage them to talk about the problems they had and how they overcame them or were overcome by them.

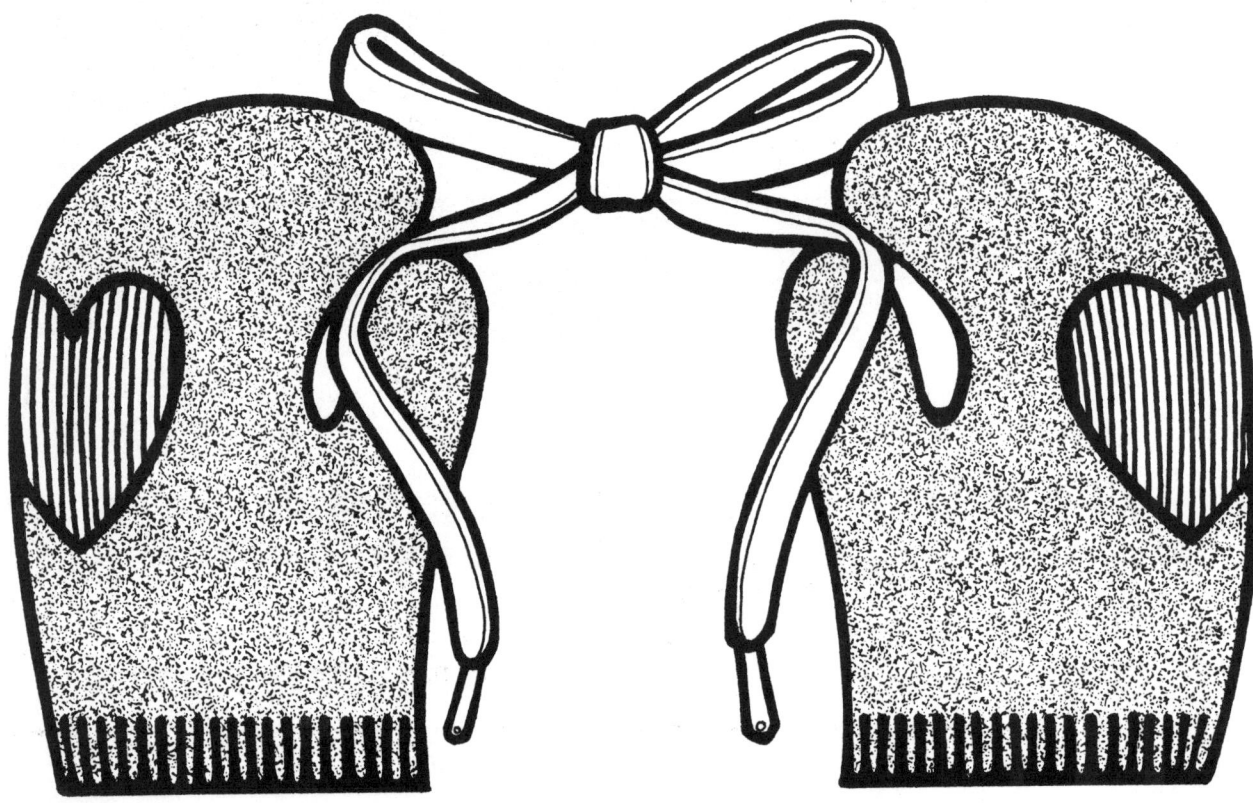

Correlated Activities
(continued)

6. Hold a wheelchair rally. Borrow wheelchairs from local rental agencies, hospitals, or special schools. Lay out a course by making a simple map of some portion of your school building and campus. Include an exterior door, hallway, classroom door, classroom aisle, water fountain, and bathroom. Have students who are *not* physically handicapped read the map and try to follow the course you have indicated in wheelchairs. Have other students walk over the same course. Record and compare their times. After the rally, encourage the students who rode in wheelchairs to describe and discuss the problems they had, the barriers they encountered, and the detours they took.

7. Use smooth, flat sticks or boards about two feet long to make splint-style leg restraints. Tie three or four sticks to each leg with bandages, handkerchiefs, or rags. Have students who are wearing the restraints walk a straight line, sit on a chair, climb stairs, and use the bathroom. Afterward, encourage them to talk about their experiences and frustrations.

8. Simulate a physical handicap such as cerebral palsy. Make restraints like the one pictured from cloth tape or webbing. Cut one strip 42 inches long and 1¼ inches wide. Cut another strip 9 inches long and 1¼ inches wide. The strips should be cut longer for children and adults.

Fold back 5½ inches at each end of the long strip and stitch down 1½ inches to make two 8-inch loops.

Attach the short strip to the long strip where one of the loops has been stitched down.

Fold up 3 inches of the short strip and stitch it to make one 6-inch loop.

To put on the finished restraint, have the child lay the long strip around his neck so that the strip goes over the right shoulder and under the left arm. Slide the free end of the long strip through the loop on the short strip. Tell the child to put his hands in the 8-inch loops at either end of the long strip. With his hands restrained close to his chest, have him do math, write, tie his shoes, or eat lunch. Make time later in the day or week for children to discuss the feelings and experiences they had while wearing the restraint.

Books, Films, and Agencies

Books for Children

Blume, Judy. *Deenie.* Scarsdale, N.Y.: Bradbury Press, 1973. Upper elementary and junior high.

Campanella, Roy. *It's Good to Be Alive.* Boston, Mass.: Little, Brown, 1959. Junior high.

Caudill, Rebecca. *Certain Small Shepherd.* New York: Holt, Rinehart and Winston, 1965. Elementary.

Davidson, Margaret. *Helen Keller.* New York: Scholastic Book Services, 1973. Primary.

———. *Louis Braille: The Boy Who Invented Books for the Blind.* New York: Hastings House, 1972. Elementary.

———. *Louis Braille: The Boy Who Invented Books for the Blind.* New York: Scholastic Book Services, 1974. Primary.

Fanshawe, Elizabeth. *Rachel.* Scarsdale, N.Y.: Bradbury Press, 1975. Primary.

Fassler, Joan. *Howie Helps Himself.* Niles, Ill.: Albert Whitman, 1975. Primary. Available from NACAC, 3900 Market Street, Suite 247, Riverside, California, 92501.

Garfield, James B. *Follow My Leader.* New York: Viking Press, 1957. Upper elementary.

Johnson, Ann Donegan. *The Value of Determination: The Story of Helen Keller.* La Jolla, Calif.: Value Communications, 1976. Elementary.

Killilea, Marie. *Karen.* Englewood Cliffs, N.J.: Prentice-Hall, 1962. Junior high, high school, and adult.

Lasker, Joe. *Nick Joins In.* Niles, Ill.: Albert Whitman, 1980. Primary.

Litchfield, Ada B. *A Cane in Her Hand.* Niles, Ill.: Albert Whitman, 1977. Primary.

Little, Jean. *Mine for Keeps.* Boston, Mass.: Little, Brown, 1962. Elementary.

Mack, Nancy. *Tracy.* Milwaukee, Wis.: Raintree Publishers, 1976. Elementary.

Putnam, Peter. *The Triumph of the Seeing Eye.* New York: Harper & Row, 1963. Upper elementary and junior high.

Raskin, Ellen. *Spectacles.* New York: Atheneum, 1972.

Savitz, Harriet May. *Fly, Wheels, Fly!* New York: Harper & Row, 1970. Junior high.

———. *On the Move.* New York: Harper & Row, 1973. Junior high.

———. *Wheelchair Champions: A History of Wheelchair Sports.* New York: Harper & Row, 1978. Upper elementary and junior high.

Stein, Sara Bonnet. *About Handicaps: An Open Family Book for Parents and Children Together.* New York: Walker, 1974. All levels.

Vance, Marguerite. *Windows for Rosemary.* New York: E. P. Dutton, 1956. Elementary.

Weiss, Malcolm E. *Blindness.* New York: Franklin Watts (a subsidiary of Grolier), 1980. Upper elementary.

Wolf, Bernard. *Connie's New Eyes.* New York: Harper & Row, 1976. Elementary, junior high, and high school.

———. *Don't Feel Sorry for Paul.* New York: Harper & Row, 1974. Elementary, junior high, and high school.

Books, Films, and Agencies
(continued)

Magazines
Disabled USA. Available free from the President's Committee on Employment of the Handicapped, 1111 Twentieth Street, N.W., Washington, D.C., 20036. Phone: (202) 653-5044.

Exceptional Children. Published by the Council for Exceptional Children, 1920 Association Drive, Reston, Virginia, 22091.

Films and Filmstrips
A Blind Teacher in a Public School. International Film Bureau.

Harold and Diana. People You'd Like to Know Series. Encyclopaedia Britannica.

Hello, Everybody. Filmstrip series available from SFA, Box 851, Pasadena, California, 91102.

How Can You Run When You Can't Even Walk? Understanding Differences Filmstrip Series. Learning Tree.

I Am Blind and *I Can't Run.* Why Am I Different Film Series. Barr Films.

Ken and *Lisa.* My New Friends Series. Eyegate.

Who Are the DeBolts, and Where Did They Get 19 Kids? Pyramid Films.

Agencies
American Council of the Blind, 1211 Connecticut Avenue, N.W., Washington, D.C., 20036.

American Foundation for the Blind, 15 West Sixteenth Street, New York, New York, 10010. Phone: (212) 924-0240.

American Printing House for the Blind, Inc., 1839 Frankfort Avenue, Louisville, Kentucky, 40206. Phone: (502) 895-2405.

Arthritis Foundation, 2113 Avenue of the Americas, New York, New York, 10036.

Boy Scouts of America, Scouting for the Handicapped Division, 1325 Walnut Hill Lane, Irving, Texas, 75062.

Directory of Organizations Interested in the Handicapped, People to People Committee for the Handicapped, Suite 1130, 1522 K Street, N.W., Washington, D.C., 20005.

Epilepsy Foundation of America, 1828 L Street, N.W., Washington, D.C., 20036.

Girl Scouts of the U.S.A., Scouting for Handicapped Girls Program, 830 Third Avenue, New York, New York, 10022.

Guide Dogs for the Blind, Inc., P.O. Box 1200, San Rafael, California, 94902. Phone: (415) 479-4000.

Library of Congress, Division for the Blind and Physically Handicapped, 1291 Taylor Street, N.W., Washington, D.C., 20542. Phone: (202) 882-5500.

Muscular Dystrophy Associations of America, Inc., 810 Seventh Avenue, New York, New York, 10019.

National Association of Sports for Cerebral Palsy, P.O. Box 3874, Amity Station, New Haven, Connecticut, 06525.

National Association of the Physically Handicapped, Inc., 6473 Grandville Avenue, Detroit, Michigan, 48228.

National Easter Seal Society for Crippled Children and Adults, 2023 West Ogden Avenue, Chicago, Illinois, 60612.

The National Foundation/March of Dimes, 1275 Mamoraneck Avenue, White Plains, New York, 10605.

National Wheelchair Athletic Association, 4024 Sixty-Second Street, Woodside, New York, 11377.

United Cerebral Palsy Association, 66 East Thirty-Fourth Street, New York, New York, 10016.

Learning Handicaps

The National Advisory Committee on Handicapped Children provides the definition most commonly used to identify children who are eligible for special learning disability services. This definition is as follows:

> Children with special learning disabilities exhibit a disorder in one or more of the basic psychological processes involved in understanding or in using spoken or written languages. These may be manifested in disorders of listening, thinking, talking, reading, writing, spelling or arithmetic. They include conditions which have been referred to as perceptual handicaps, brain injury, minimal brain dysfunction, dyslexia, developmental aphasia, etc. They do not include learning problems which are due primarily to visual, hearing, or motor handicaps, to mental retardation, emotional disturbance, or to environmental disadvantage.

Learning disabilities, or disorders, can be divided into six categories. These categories are motor activity, emotionality, perception, symbolization, attention, and memory.

Children with **disorders of motor activity** may be hyperactive or hypoactive and may exhibit incoordination or perseveration. **Hyperactive** children are always moving, often randomly and erratically. **Hypoactive** children are quiet and lethargic. **Incoordination** is physical awkwardness in activities such as running and skipping, writing and drawing. It is often characterized by a rigid gait, stumbling, and generally clumsy behavior. **Perseveration** is the automatic and involuntary continuation of behavior.

Perceptual disorders are distinguished from sensory defects such as blindness and deafness. Children with perceptual disorders can see and hear but have difficulty organizing and interpreting the physical elements of stimuli. In school, they may reverse letters and numbers or be unable to distinguish figure from background.

Children with **symbolization disorders** have difficulty associating symbols with the concepts or ideas for which they stand. Children with **attention disorders** are unable to focus and then break attention when appropriate.

In most public schools, children with learning disabilities are placed in regular classrooms but receive individualized instruction from a resource specialist.

Learning Handicaps
Bulletin Board Idea

Riddles, Riddles

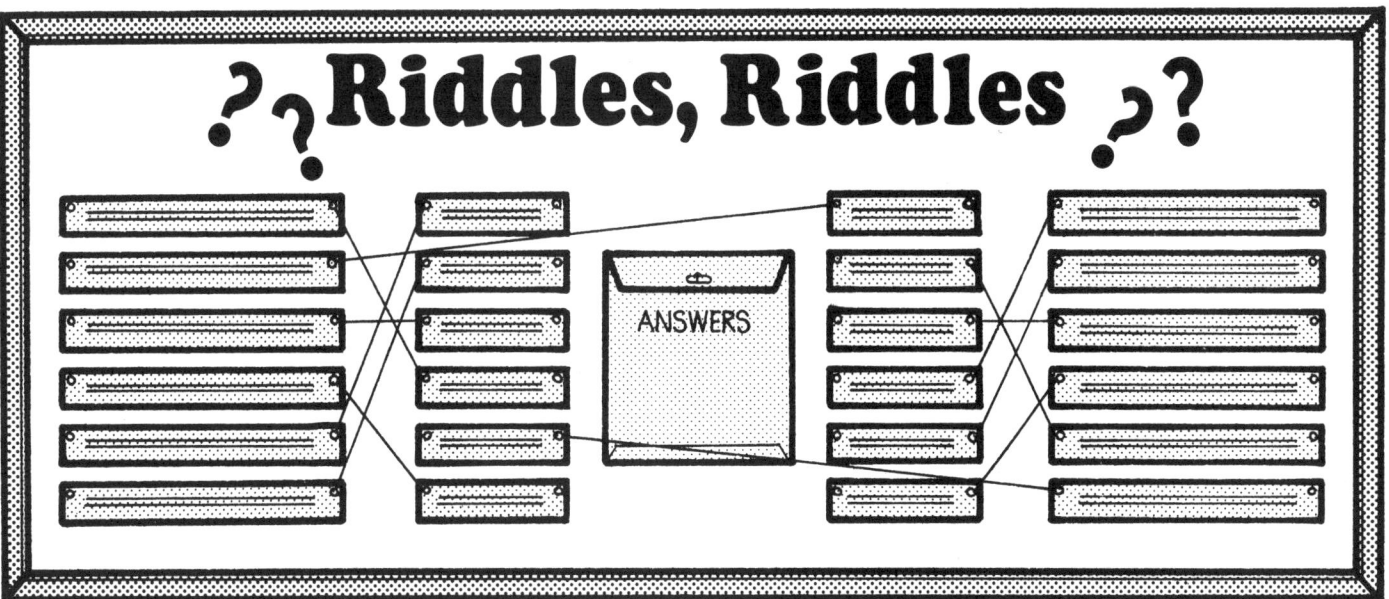

What You Need

- paper letters to spell **Riddles, Riddles**
- paper question marks
- Riddle and Answer Strips on page 56
- scissors
- colored construction paper, tagboard, or index cards
- glue
- clear Contact paper (optional)
- lengths of bright-colored yarn
- thumbtacks or map tacks
- a clasp envelope or manila file folder

What You Do

1. Make two copies of page 56.
2. Leave one copy intact to serve as an answer key.
3. Cut the Riddle and Answer Strips on the other copy apart.
4. Glue the strips to colored construction paper, tagboard, or plain index cards.
5. To make the strips more durable, laminate them or cover them with clear Contact paper.
6. Post the letters, question marks, riddles, and answers on the board.
7. With tacks, attach a length of yarn to one corner of each riddle card.
8. Put the answer key in a clasp envelope or manila folder and attach it securely to the board.
9. Make additional tacks available on or near the board.
10. Encourage students to go to the riddle board and match riddles with answers by connecting them with yarn. When they have finished making the connections, tell them to check their matches against those given on the answer key.

Variations

- To make the board more challenging, do *not* post the answers. Supply cards and let students guess the answers, print their guesses on the cards, and post the cards on the board. Mark the correct answers with yarn.
- Use questions from a particular subject or skill area or riddles on a single theme.
- Challenge students to write the answers as a perceptually handicapped person might. (See page 61).

We All Come In Different Packages
©1983—The Learning Works, Inc.

Riddle and Answer Strips

Riddle: If you were surrounded by twenty lions, fifteen tigers, and ten leopards, how would you get away from them?	**Answer:** Ask the merry-go-round operator to stop it so you could get off.
Riddle: Every morning Farmer Brown had eggs for breakfast; but he didn't own any chickens, and he never got eggs from chickens owned by anyone else. Where did he get the eggs?	**Answer:** From his ducks. He ate ducks' eggs.
Riddle: I have cities without houses, forests without trees, and rivers without water. What am I?	**Answer:** A map.
Riddle: What is it that every child spends much time making, yet no one can ever see after it has been made?	**Answer:** Noise.
Riddle: What can you break as easily with a whisper as with a hammer?	**Answer:** Silence.
Riddle: Why is a river rich?	**Answer:** Because it always has two banks.
Riddle: How do you know that flowers are lazy?	**Answer:** You always find them in beds.
Riddle: What must be broken before it can be used?	**Answer:** An egg.
Riddle: What age is served for breakfast?	**Answer:** Sausage.
Riddle: What can you put in your right hand but not in your left hand?	**Answer:** Your left elbow.
Riddle: What lives in winter, dies in summer, and grows with its roots upward?	**Answer:** An icicle.
Riddle: Who are the best bookkeepers?	**Answer:** People who never return the books they borrow.

I'm proud of myself when I do things my way.

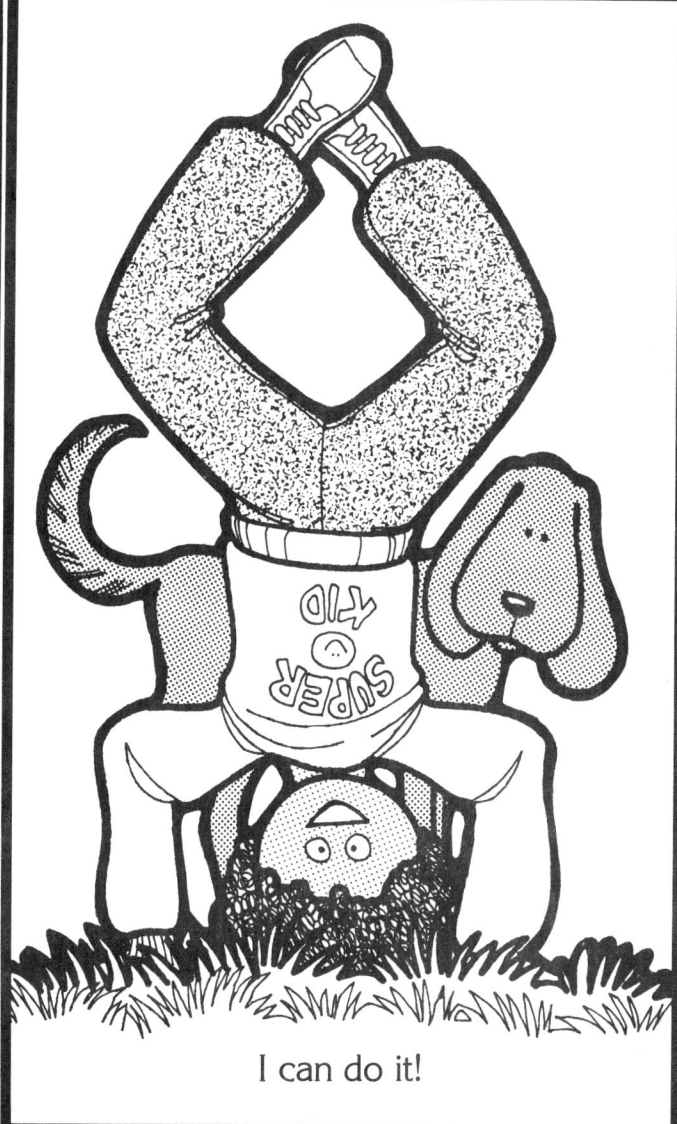

I can do it!

Relaxing feels good.

Learning Handicaps
Mini-Posters

We All Come In Different Packages
©1983—The Learning Works, Inc.

Learning Handicaps
Individual Activity Sheet

Name _____

Fun with Words

The eighteen terms listed at the bottom of this page are used to talk and write about learning handicaps.

1. Find these terms hidden in the puzzle. Remember to look from left to right, from right to left, from top to bottom, from bottom to top, and along the diagonal.
2. Put these terms in alphabetical order.
3. Choose five of these terms. Look them up in a dictionary or encyclopedia. Find out how to say them, what they mean, and what they have to do with learning disabilities.

```
Y C O N C E P T U A L I Z A T I O N V T E I R A T E H
T A N O O T D E C O D I N G L S Q O G T G C M A P H A
I Z A V H I R I S K A P L O T O A P I N I A H O E I N
V O M W K L W G W S T E N I H A E O V I D I L T C N D
I S P E C I A L C L A S S I M C L T L D N X S A N C E
T L O L T A H N T L A D B O N O Y H W A E E I S O T D
C M F N W E T I G B A Y G O G E T L O I M L S X C S N
A T N N S O A I K R A M M Y G S I C R E A S E O F A E
R O N E M O T I O N A L L A B I L I T Y R Y S A L D S
E N O G H E H T U O F M X P U T A W O R K D P E E V S
P P I I O S I R T L Y B M L K I D K I N D L E S S O T
Y L T R G I N G E R S N A P S C O L O R C O D I N G B
H A I L B R E S O U R C E R O O M V R X Z K J F W Q B
E Z N S H E S C B S N I Y T I L I B I T C A R T S I D
F I G U R E G R O U N D G G O N D I N R A D T L T H E
R I O N W C I R S A T V P A I L U C L A C S Y D E M T
E N C O D I N G I C B Z O L A V G R A M M A R L K M O
```

decoding
emotional lability
grammar
resource room
special class
handedness

encoding
distractibility
cognition
self-concept
modality
hyperactivity

color coding
conceptualization
dyslexia
dyscalculia
figure-ground
etiology

We All Come In Different Packages
©1983—The Learning Works, Inc.

Learning Handicaps
Individual Activity Sheet

Name _____

Can You Follow Directions?

Some children with learning handicaps have trouble understanding what they read and following written directions. Even though they try very hard, they get mixed up and may not be able to do something as fast as other children can do it.

See how well you follow directions. Ask your teacher or a friend to time you. You have three minutes to read and follow the directions on this page.

1. Read everything before doing anything.
2. Print your name on the line in the upper right-hand corner of this page.
3. Circle the word **name** in sentence 2.
4. Draw five small squares in the lower right-hand corner of this page.
5. Put an **X** in each square.
6. Put a small circle around each square.
7. Sign your name under the title of this page.
8. After the title write, "Yes, yes, yes."
9. Put a circle around sentence number 7.
10. Put an **X** in the lower left-hand corner of the page.
11. Draw a triangle around this **X**.
12. On the other side of this paper, add 236 and 435.
13. Draw a circle around the word **page** in sentence 4.
14. Raise the hand you don't write with and go on to number 15.
15. Put your arithmetic book on top of your desk.
16. On the other side of this paper, subtract 79 from 97.
17. Put a circle around your printed name and a square around the circle.
18. Underline all of the even numbers on this page.
19. Say out loud, "I am nearly finished. I have followed directions."
20. Now that you have finished reading carefully, do only sentences one and two.

We All Come In Different Packages
©1983—The Learning Works, Inc.

Learning Handicaps
Individual Activity Sheet

Name _____

Following Directions

Some children with learning handicaps have trouble understanding what they read because their brains mix up the letters.

The letters in the directions below are already mixed up. Your brain will have to straighten them out. You have three minutes to read each sentence carefully and do what it says.

1. Print your name in cabital sretlel ni the ubber rig4t-4anb corner fo a diece fo baber.

2. Unbern̄eat4 ti, bram a cirlce t4at si 3 inc4ez ni biawet̄er.

3. In t4e mibble fo t4e bage, bram a zquare t4at meazurez 6 inc4ez no eac4 zibe.

4. W4en you 4ave finiz4eb, raize your 4anb.

Learning Handicaps
Group Activity Sheet

Aren't You Finished Yet?

Purpose

If timed right, this activity allows more able children to experience firsthand some of the frustrations frequently experienced by their less able or learning disabled classmates when they are forced to work under pressure or against unreasonable deadlines. It helps all children understand and appreciate individual differences.

What You Need

- the math worksheet on page 63 or any other similar worksheet that is appropriate for your class
- a timer with a bell or other audible signal (preferably one that ticks loudly)
- pencils for all class members

What You Do

1. Make enough copies of the worksheet so that every class member can have one.
2. Hand a worksheet face down to each student.
3. Caution students *not* to turn over their papers and begin work until you tell them to do so.
4. Explain to students that, as they do the worksheet, they will be working against time, and urge them emphatically to work as quickly as possible.
5. Set the timer for *half* of the time you think most class members will need to complete the worksheet.
6. Tell students to turn over their papers and begin.
7. As students work, alternately ask how many are finished and tell them how little time they have left. Every now and then, ask in an exasperated and incredulous tone, "Aren't you finished yet?"
8. When the timer sounds, tell students to stop work immediately, put down their pencils, and turn over their papers.
9. Ask those who finished to raise their hands.
10. Ask those who did *not* finish to raise their hands.
11. Express surprise and, in a tone of shock and disbelief, ask some specific members of this latter group *why* they did not finish.
12. Pause for a moment and then confess that the exercise was not really fair. Explain that you intentionally allowed students less time than you thought they would need and kept nagging them about time so that they would have trouble concentrating.
13. Now that you have been honest with the children, encourage them to be honest with you about how they felt during the exercise. Did they feel pressured and frustrated? Help them to realize and understand that we all work comfortably at different paces. Some children, especially those with learning handicaps, need more time than others to do their work and complete assignments. Ask, *How would you feel if you thought that you never could finish your work on time? Would you keep trying anyway?*

We All Come In Different Packages
©1983—The Learning Works, Inc.

Aren't You Finished Yet?

	a	b	c	d	e
1	0 + 0	5 − 2	3 + 6	5 0 + 1	4 3 + 2
2	42 + 7	65 + 14	37 + 11	56 + 2	103 + 25
3	4 + 3	92 + 1	45 − 21	42 13 + 50	14 91 + 4
4	45 + 21	29 − 18	75 + 8	23 − 3	32 24 + 40
5	75 + 11	44 + 19	44 − 19	17 10 + 41	34 43 + 13
6	75 − 21	67 + 43	27 + 38	96 − 84	61 − 15
7	76 − 28	47 − 26	61 − 15	72 + 50	53 + 68

Learning Handicaps
Group Activity Sheet

Mirror Writing

Purpose

Some people with handicaps perceive things differently. Their brains have trouble organizing and interpreting visual stimuli. Objects in one place may appear to them to be in another, completely different, place. The lines and shapes that make up letters and numbers may look backwards or be reversed. This activity helps children understand how confusing such misinterpretation can be.

What You Need

- the Double-Line Star on page 65
- a mirror
- a piece of cardboard
- pencils

What You Do

1. Make enough copies of the Double-Line Star on page 65 so that each class member can have one.
2. Place one copy of the star on a desk or table.
3. Attach the mirror securely to a board or wall behind the desk.
4. Make pencils available.
5. Hold or place a piece of cardboard so that students working at the desk will not be able to see their hands.
6. Tell students to come to the desk one at a time to draw and write.

What Students Do

1. Look in the mirror, *not* at your hands.
2. Write your name on the name line at the top of the page.
3. Trace between the lines of the double star.
4. On the lines at the bottom of the page, write a message for a friend to read.

Related Activity

- Talk with children about how they felt when their hands seemed to go the wrong way. Help them understand that children with learning disabilities, for whom drawing and writing are difficult, have similar feelings.

We All Come In Different Packages
©1983—The Learning Works, Inc.

Learning Handicaps
Individual Activity Sheet

Name _____

Double-Line Star

_____

_____

_____

We All Come In Different Packages
©1983—The Learning Works, Inc.

Colin's Story

Purpose
The purpose of this activity is to help children understand how it feels to be "different."

What You Need
- Colin's Story on page 67

What You Do
1. Read the introduction on this page and then explain to your students who Colin is.
2. Read Colin's story to students or let them read it themselves.
3. Use the questions below as the basis for small-group or whole-class discussions or for written assignments.

Introduction
Colin Corbett Ruffner is the sixteen-year-old son of Robert H. Ruffner, director of communications for the President's Committee on Employment of the Handicapped. Colin told his story in his own words. He wanted people to understand not how others feel about a person with a learning disability but rather how it feels to be the person whose life is affected by the decisions those "others" make.

As Colin conscientiously explains, he is not an expert on learning disability; but his sensitive, candid statement about his life and his feelings gives us a glimpse of what we too frequently miss—the human being who is waiting behind the statistics we too often see.

Questions
1. What was Colin's problem?
2. How did Colin's problem make him feel?
3. How did his feelings make him act?
4. Was his behavior choice a good one or a bad one for him? Why do you think so?
5. What else might Colin have done?
6. Are there some ways Colin might have helped himself?
7. What did Colin's parents do to help?
8. Why weren't they successful?
9. After reading the story, do you think Colin had very many friends? Why or why not?
10. What could Colin's friends have done to help him?
11. Do you know a boy or girl like Colin?
12. What can you do to help him or her?
13. If Colin came to your school now, would things go better for him than they did then? Why or why not?

Colin's Story

I must first state that I am not an expert on learning disability. I have had only one contact with it, and that's myself. So my reasons may not apply to everyone, and my story may not be the same in that light.

I have had what I consider a pretty hard school life so far. I can't honestly say that I've had a whole lot of fun. I blame a lot of things. First off, now it has become all right for all types of people, groups, and so on to come out of the "closet." But during the most important years of my school life, 1966 to 1977, it was not all right to be different.

I could not read or write in the fifth grade. I was always in trouble. The schools just plain blamed me, and, of course, my folks. But my mother and dad supported and helped me.

My parents went to meeting after meeting looking for help with all sorts of "pros." Always the same answer: "Colin has just a few problems, nothing that a good doctor can't fix."

Well, during all of this time, I felt horrible. They—meaning the schools—didn't want me in their classes because they didn't have enough time for me. The old "Why worry about him when little Jack and Ann are doing so well?"

Well, to make myself feel like someone, I had to pick a role, with a make-believe world. I made myself into the meanest, baddest little fifth-grader you've ever seen. And it went on for a number of years, until it got so that even I believed it. Of course, this led to getting into trouble with school people and even with the police. The midnight knock on the front door.

With all this, I was in and out of just about every "special" school around. And finally I was back in public school. Which only meant more trouble and, of course, a very big nasty reputation which goes along with all of this.

Then I took the big step and quit school. I refused to go to another "special" school, and I refused to beg my way back into the public schools. Now, I'm between schools or "lost in the cracks."

Colin's Story is reprinted by permission from *Disabled USA*, vol. 2, no. 5, pp. 3-7.

The only other thing that I can say about all of this is that I hope, with the new understanding and point of view that people have of learning disability today and with the new tolerance of people who aren't like everyone else, that the Billys, Marys, Tommys, and Sues, and their parents won't have to go through the nightmare that myself and my family have been through.

Postscript: Colin has since passed the general educational development (GED) test and attends a community college.

Learning Handicaps
Additional Activity Ideas

Correlated Activities

1. On construction paper or tagboard strips, write sentences in which there are common perceptual errors. Provide cutouts so that children can correct these errors.

    > I am ƨab.   I am [sad].

2. **Mainstreaming** means integrating students with mental and physical handicaps into the public schools. State and private welfare agencies have developed similar programs to integrate adults with handicaps into the mainstream of society. Have students write essays in which they explore the concept of mainstreaming in schools and in society. Propose that they use their essays to answer such questions as, *How do you feel about mainstreaming? What are the benefits for people with handicaps? What are the benefits for society as a whole? What are some of the problems that must be solved before this approach becomes truly workable? What solutions would you suggest?*

3. Many famous people have had recognized communicative, physical, and learning handicaps. Among them are the following:

Jane Addams	Homer
Ludwig van Beethoven	Helen Keller
Sarah Bernhardt	Guglielmo Marconi
Miguel de Cervantes	Joseph Pulitzer
Moshe Dayan	Franklin Delano Roosevelt
Thomas Alva Edison	Charles Steinmetz
Albert Einstein	James Thurber
Rex Harrison	Henri de Toulouse-Lautrec

    Have students choose one of these people and do research to learn (1) the nature of the handicap, (2) how the handicap affected the life of the person, and (3) what the person accomplished despite the handicap. Suggest that students share what they have learned by giving oral reports or writing short skits and presenting them to the class. Students might work in groups of two or three to prepare and present their skits.

4. Have students build a wall of myths about handicaps and people who have them. Cut bricks from construction paper. On each brick, write a myth. Use the myths listed on pages 14-17 or others of which you are aware. Attach these bricks to a wall with masking tape. Remove the bricks one by one as students discover the truth.

5. Have students cut out stars or some other complicated shape with their nonpreferred hands. After the activity ask, *Did you do a good job? Are you proud of your work? Is it as good as you would like for it to be? How do you think students with perceptual problems feel when their work is not as good as they would like it to be?*

Learning Handicaps
Resource List

Books, Films, and Agencies

Books for Children

Albert, Louise. *But I'm Ready to Go.* Scarsdale, N.Y.: Bradbury Press, 1976. Upper elementary, junior high, and high school.

Glazzard, Margaret H. *Meet Scott: Learning Disabled.* Lawrence, Kans.: H & H Enterprises, 1978. Primary.

Hayes, Marnell. *Tuned-in, Turned-on Book About Learning Problems.* Novato, Calif.: Academic Therapy, 1974. Upper elementary.

Hunter, Edith F. *Sue Ellen.* Boston, Mass.: Houghton Mifflin, 1969. Elementary.

Kraus, Robert. *Leo the Late Bloomer.* New York: Windmill Books, 1971. Primary.

Lasker, Joe. *He's My Brother.* Niles, Ill.: Albert Whitman, 1974. Primary.

Pevsner, Stella. *Keep Stompin' Till the Music Stops.* Boston, Mass.: Houghton Mifflin, 1976. Upper elementary.

———. *Keep Stompin' Till the Music Stops.* New York: Scholastic Book Services, 1979. Upper elementary.

Smith, Doris B. *Kelly's Creek.* New York: Harper & Row, 1975. Upper elementary.

Films and Filmstrips

Chesler, E. A. *A Walk in Another Pair of Shoes.* California Association for Neurologically Handicapped Children, 1972. Eighteen-minute color filmstrip with tape.

Hello, Everybody. Filmstrip series available from SFA, Box 851, Pasadena, California, 91102.

Kids Come in Special Flavors. Classroom kit available from Kids Come in Special Flavors Company, Box 562, Forest Park Station, Dayton, Ohio, 45405.

Agencies

California Association for Neurologically Handicapped Children, 645 Odlin Drive, Pleasant Hill, California, 94523.

Council for Exceptional Children (CEC), 1920 Association Drive, Reston, Virginia, 22091. Phone: (800) 336-3728.

Association for Children with Learning Disabilities (ACLD), 4156 Library Road, Pittsburgh, Pennsylvania, 15234. Phone: (412) 341-1515.

Mental Handicaps

Mental retardation is less-than-normal intellectual function. It may be caused by genetic defect, as in Down's syndrome, or by environmental causes, such as prenatal malnutrition, infection, or prematurity.

There are four recognized degrees of mental retardation: mild, moderate, severe, and profound. Adults who are mildly retarded usually can support themselves and be independent. Adults who are moderately retarded can work in sheltered workshops. Adults who are severely retarded may be able to feed and dress themselves. People who are profoundly retarded need others to care for them.

More than six million people in the United States are retarded. Most of them are mildly retarded.

Mental Handicaps
Bulletin Board Idea

Hello, I'm Retarded

What You Need

- photographs or drawings of a boy and a girl
- paper letters to spell **Hello, I'm Retarded**
- a large piece of butcher paper, tagboard, or construction paper

What You Do

1. Post the pictures and letters on the board.
2. Print the message written above or a similar one on the piece of butcher paper, tagboard, or construction paper.
3. Add the finished message to the board.

Related Activities

- Discuss mental retardation with class members. Help them to understand that the mentally retarded person has a real problem, not a make-believe one, that mentally retarded people cannot "help" being retarded, and that their condition is not contagious.
- During class discussion, elicit suggestions of ways to help a mentally retarded person and list them on the chalkboard.
- Role play situations involving mentally retarded people. It may be useful at first to have some knowledgeable adult (a school counselor, aide, or parent) play the role of the retarded person.

Mental Handicaps
Mini-Posters

We All Come In Different Packages
©1983—The Learning Works, Inc.

72

Mental Handicaps
Mini-Posters

Handicapped children are children first.

I'm not sure where I'm going, but I'm off to a good start.

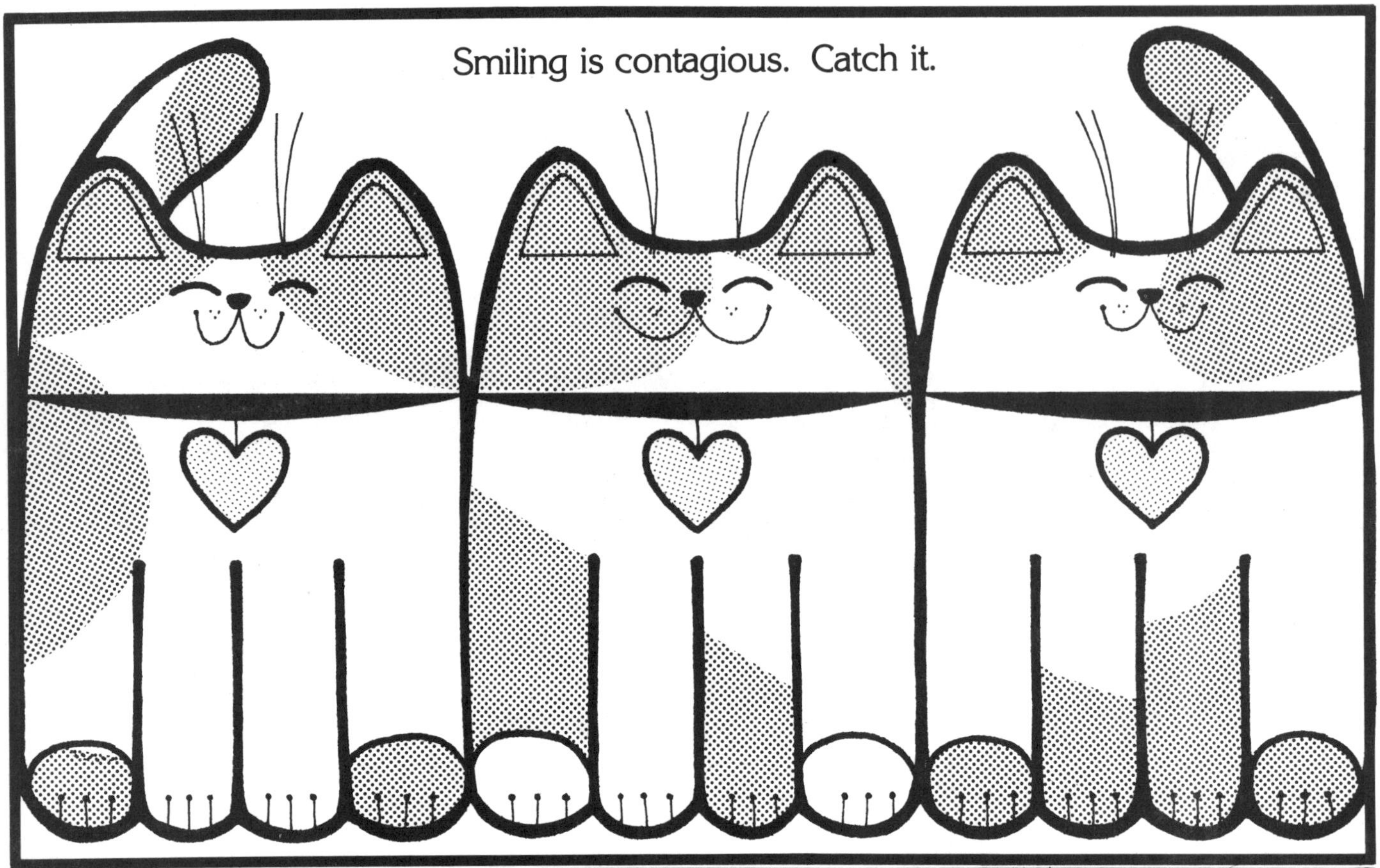

Mental Handicaps
Mini-Posters

Smiling is contagious. Catch it.

Do something kind for someone special today.

We All Come In Different Packages
©1983—The Learning Works, Inc.

Mental Handicaps
Individual Activity Sheet

Name _____

Fun with Words

The thirteen terms listed at the bottom of this page are used to talk and write about mental retardation and the things that cause it.

1. Find these terms hidden in the puzzle. Remember to look from left to right, from right to left, from top to bottom, from bottom to top, and along the diagonal.
2. Put these terms in alphabetical order.
3. Choose five of these terms. Look them up in a dictionary or encyclopedia. Find out how to say them, what they mean, and what they have to do with mental retardation.

```
K M Z P B F O A K D F G L A J I R Q D I P Y O I O F L
L S P E C I A L O L Y M P I C S N B G M M O V N T E I
X A X U T P B R K S W X T X B A E M C D F R I E B B O
T S D O R S F T D E V E L O P M E N T N B W W A K N T
A V W X Z I G E V M E N I N G I T I S A R O L N O W I
P N O I T A D R A T E R L A T N E M Q T A S C H L I F
D E V E L O P M E N T A L D I S A B I L I T Y Y T O S
M I T O P S N H D P C P D A I M I T E M N N L D W S N
I Q U I V O A I C O N G E N I T A L S N E R O R H E L
V S K T D B O C N G B A K D O W N S S Y N D R O M E L
T A C H T A L L E B U R Y R I B Z E M G H E G C W S O
O K W Z M C H R O M O S O M E N W H O L I K E E O A C
Y G E B E O Y S R H H C U B D O I W G M L T I P N H V
H N I H F U U H A E I A S T G M F E T U S O R H K C W
L U S K N G S O E R M L I G E N E S N K T E A A T B Z
M T H C T I N U L T G E A T E F Y N E O H L I L N P D
S E A R E A R L D K T O V S M O U K R Y G Y D Y O J P
```

      bond IQ
     anoxia fetus
     rubella mislabel
    meningitis development
  Down's syndrome hydrocephaly
 mental retardation special olympics
   developmental disability

Mental Handicaps
Group Activity Sheet

Tom's Story

Purpose

The purpose of this activity is to help children understand that mentally retarded people can learn to do many things and have the same emotional needs other people have.

What You Need

- Tom's story on pages 77-78

What You Do

1. Reproduce enough copies of pages 77 and 78 so that each member of the class can have one copy of each page.
2. Hand out the copies.
3. Read Tom's story to the children or let them read it themselves.
4. Use the questions on page 78 as a written lesson or as the basis for a discussion of the story.

Additional Discussion Questions

1. What is Down's syndrome? Is it a disease or a condition? What causes it? Is it contagious? Can it be cured? Can someone who has it be helped? How?
2. What do you want to do when you grow up? Do you think that Tom could learn to do that? Why or why not?
3. Do you have a friend like Tom? If so, tell about your friend. Share some of your experiences with the class.

Mental Handicaps
Individual Activity Sheet

Name _____

Tom's Story

Tom is a seventeen-year-old high school student. He rides the bus with other high school kids, carries an identification card, and works part time at McDonald's. He lives in Anywhere, USA. His name has been changed, but his story is real.

Tom has Down's syndrome, and he is retarded. He could have grown up in an institution, but his parents wanted him to be part of their family, just like their other children. Tom's parents felt that their family's love and care would help Tom learn more and be happier than if he lived in an institution.

Even when Tom was a tiny baby, his brothers and sisters knew that he needed their help. One of the boys taught Tom to shake hands. He would walk up to Tom's crib and say, "Shake, pal." The other children taught Tom to walk. The whole family worked together to teach Tom to do the things that they believed he could learn to do.

Tom is a teen-ager, not a child. Sometimes it's easy to treat Tom and other mentally handicapped people like children, but Tom doesn't want to be treated that way. He doesn't want to be completely dependent on others. He has learned to be independent. He makes his own decisions about what he will do with his life. He wants to be treated as an individual.

Tom goes to a special class in a regular high school. He has friends in his neighborhood who go to the same school. He eats in the cafeteria with the other kids and joins them for physical education classes. He cracks jokes like other teen-agers. He goes to the store and buys his own things.

Tom's confidence has grown so much that he went to McDonald's and got a job on his own. He does such a good job that his boss is interested in hiring other handicapped workers.

Even though Tom is retarded, his emotional needs are the same as everyone else's. He needs affection, recognition, and understanding. Those needs are filled for Tom in his home, in his school, and in his job.

Mental Handicaps
Individual Activity Sheet

Name _____

Tom's Story
(continued)

After you have read "Tom's Story," answer the following questions by writing the correct words on the lines.

1. How old is Tom? _____
2. Where does Tom live? _____
3. Is this a real place? _____
4. What does it mean or stand for? _____
   _____
5. Is Tom's story real? _____
6. How do you know? _____
7. What's wrong with Tom? _____
   _____
8. Look up the word **institution** in a dictionary. Notice that it has several meanings. What does it mean in this story? _____
   _____
9. Did Tom's family decide to keep him at home or to put him in an institution?
   _____
10. Why did they make this decision? _____
    _____
11. What does the story say Tom's brothers and sisters taught him to do when he was a baby?
    _____
12. What other things do you think Tom's family taught him? _____
    _____
13. Now that Tom has grown up, what things can he do? _____
    _____
14. What three emotional needs does Tom share with everyone else? _____
    _____

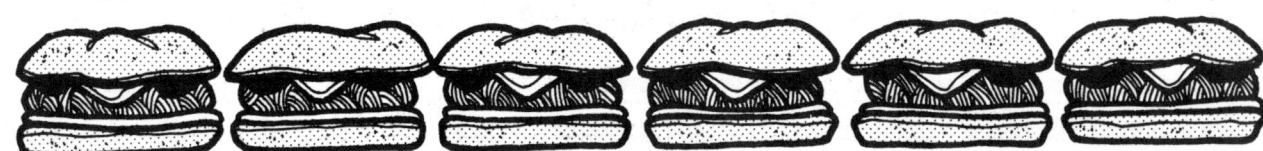

We All Come In Different Packages
©1983—The Learning Works, Inc.

Mental Handicaps
Group Activity Sheet

Smarties and Slowpokes

Purpose

The purpose of this activity is to help children realize that things aren't always what they seem: things that *look* easy may actually *be* difficult, and things that appear to be impossible may actually be quite simple, once you have been given all of the instructions and understand what you are to do.

What You Need

- worksheets on pages 80 and 81
- pencils

What You Do

1. Reproduce enough copies of the worksheets on pages 80 and 81 so that every member of your class can have one copy of each sheet.
2. Arbitrarily divide the class into two equal groups designated Group I and Group II.
3. Send the members of Group II out of the room.
4. Hand out copies of Sheet I to the members of Group I.
5. Tell them to read their worksheets, underline every third word, read only the underlined words, and follow the instructions. Caution them *not* to talk or to give any hints to the members of Group II.
6. Have the members of Group II return.
7. Give them copies of Sheet I.
8. Tell them only that they are to read and follow the instructions. Give no additional explanation or help.
9. Allow a set period of time for the members of both groups to work.
10. When time is up, collect the worksheets.
11. Send the members of Group I out of the room.
12. Hand out copies of Sheet II to the members of Group II.
13. Tell them to read their worksheets carefully, underline every third word, and then read the underlined words backward (from end to beginning, bottom to top), and follow the instructions. Caution them *not* to talk or to give any hints to the members of Group I.
14. Have the members of Group I return.
15. Give them copies of Sheet II.
16. Tell them only that they are to read and follow the instructions. Give no additional explanation or help.
17. Allow a set period of time for the members of both groups to work.
18. When time is up, collect the worksheets.
19. Initiate a discussion of this activity. Ask such questions as, *Were you able to follow the instructions and do the activity? How did you feel when the instructions didn't seem to work? How did you feel when the work seemed difficult for you but easy for someone else? Do you think mentally retarded students have feelings similar to the ones you have described?*

Smarties and Slowpokes, Sheet I

1. Horse seven draw orange desk a cat dog circle this that the big elephant size up down of off paper a football milk tennis circle cut ball house monkey on him paste this pig pot page.

2. The boy draw ran home a big dark smaller blue house circle here away on grass school top house cat of on no the farm animal first.

3. Day comes draw after night a and then funny we go hat now play on yellow chair top one bird of ball cut the little big smaller girl are circle.

4. Grandmother say draw window in a on have face this time in purple ten the room bed smaller hand over circle.

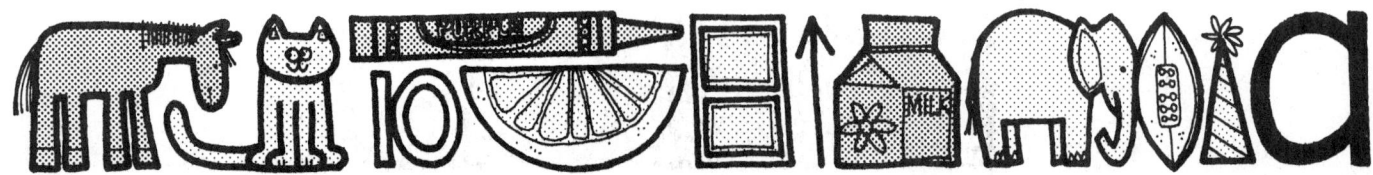

Smarties and Slowpokes, Sheet II

1. Girls can name the seven teacher's books if your desk can underline black pencils.

2. Boys can number the white room and at your short school around those people circle big box a six or put shoes here.

3. Give a name to your teacher's dog if your feet are above the highest number in your room and if your dog can write.

4. Look on page one is the very best of the whole bottom row if the new one at school with name of my teacher's pet was your friend will write the letter.

Mental Handicaps
Additional Activity Ideas

Correlated Activities

1. Divide the chalkboard into two columns. Head one column **Ways We Are Alike,** and head the other column **Ways We Are Different.** Have normal children think of ways in which they are like mentally retarded children and ways in which they are different from them. For example, entries under **Ways We Are Alike** might read *We both like hamburgers, We both need love,* and *We both need help sometimes.* Emphasize that retarded children are like children of normal intelligence in all ways except intellectual function.

2. Have students list and/or create some games that would be suitable to play with mentally retarded children. These games should have few instructions or rules and should involve simple actions or motions that can be learned once and then repeated over and over again.

3. Have students think of ways to simplify the rules of several favorite games so that they will be less complex and easier for mentally retarded children to learn and follow.

4. If possible, arrange to visit a school, class, or home for mentally retarded children to sing songs, play games, or put on a short program.

5. Invite a group of mentally retarded students to visit your classroom. Use your thinking from Activities 2 and 3 above as you plan activities and choose games to enjoy with your guests. Avoid competition, especially between handicapped and nonhandicapped. Assign each visiting mentally retarded child a partner with normal intellectual function. Emphasize cooperation.

6. Arrange ahead of time with the teacher of a mentally handicapped class to have your class and her class draw pictures and/or write poems on a similar theme. Exchange the resulting student work temporarily, and exhibit the poems or artwork for students to enjoy. If appropriate, print some observations and/or conclusions on strips of tagboard or construction paper, and add them to the exhibit. For example, you might write, *All of us like snow, All of us enjoy sports,* or *All of us look forward to special holidays.*

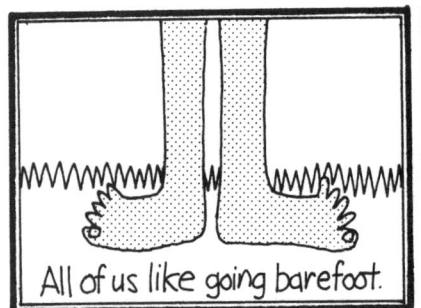

Books, Films, and Agencies

Books for Children
Brightman, Alan. *Like Me.* Boston, Mass.: Little, Brown, 1976. Primary.
Brown, Helene. *Yesterday's Child.* New York: M. Evans, 1976.
Byars, Betsy. *The Summer of the Swans.* New York: Avon Books, 1974. Upper elementary.
Cleaver, Vera, and Bill Cleaver. *Me, Too.* New York: Harper & Row, 1973. Upper elementary.
Keyes, Daniel. *Flowers for Algernon.* New York: Harcourt Brace Jovanovich, 1966.
Smith, Gene. *The Hayburners.* New York: Delacorte Press, 1974. Junior high.
Sobol, Harriet L. *My Brother Steven Is Retarded.* New York: Macmillan, 1977. Upper elementary.
Spence, Eleanor. *The Nothing Place.* New York: Harper & Row, 1973. Upper elementary and junior high.
Steinbeck, John. *Of Mice and Men.* New York: Penguin Books, 1978. High school.

Films and Filmstrips
Charly. Color, 103 minutes. High school.
Dream to Grow on 1968. Arlington, Tex.: National Association for Retarded Citizens.
He's Mentally Retarded. Color, 8 minutes. Elementary.
Hello, Everybody. Filmstrip series available from SFA, Box 851, Pasadena, California, 91102.
Kids Come in Special Flavors. Classroom kit available from the Kids Come in Special Flavors Company, Box 562, Forest Park Station, Dayton, Ohio, 45405.
Of Mice and Men. 110 minutes. High school.
People You'd Like to Know Series. Encyclopaedia Britannica.
Understanding Differences Filmstrip Series. Learning Tree.

Agencies
Council for Exceptional Children (CEC), 1920 Association Drive, Reston, Virginia, 22091. Phone: (800) 336-3728.
Down's Syndrome Congress, 1802 Johnson Drive, Normal, Illinois, 61761.
National Association of Retarded Citizens (NARC), 2709 Avenue E East, P.O. Box 6109, Arlington, Texas, 76011.
Special Olympics, 719 Thirteenth Street, N.W., Suite 510, Washington, D.C., 20005.

Glossary

anoxia	a lack of oxygen which can cause permanent damage to the deprived part of the body
Apgar scale	a checklist devised by Dr. Virginia Apgar to allow rapid assessment of a newborn baby's physical condition so that potential problem areas can be quickly identified and monitored
bond	the strong emotional connection that develops between an infant and those who care for him and is necessary to promote a feeling of security and of belonging
Braille	a raised-dot alphabet devised by Louis Braille which makes it possible for blind people to read with their fingertips
brain	the large, soft mass of tissue located inside the skull which is the seat of consciousness and controls most of the rest of the body
chromosome	a microscopic, rodlike, chromatin-containing basophilic body found in relatively constant numbers in the cells of any one kind of plant or animal. Human beings have 46 (or 23 pairs) of chromosomes in each cell. Chromosomal abnormalities may result in diseases or defects. For example, **Down's syndrome**, or mongolism, occurs when failure of the twenty-first chromosome to divide properly yields three chromosomes in this position instead of the expected pair. This condition is called **trisomy-21**.
cognition	the act or process of knowing as distinguished from feeling; the intellectual process by which one gains knowledge
color coding	a teaching technique in which related items are similarly colored to help the learner recognize the relationships and learn more rapidly
concept	an idea, thought, or notion conceived in the mind
conceptualize	to form concepts; to have thoughts or ideas
conceptualization	the act or process of forming concepts and having thoughts or ideas
congenital	existing or dating from birth
congenital disability	a handicap or disabling condition that exists at birth because of something that happened to the fetus in the womb and that may or may not be hereditary
decibel	unit used to measure the relative loudness of sounds
decoding	the act or process of interpreting received stimuli and understanding received messages; interpreting or understanding what has been expressed
development	the complicated process that results in physical growth, mental understanding, and emotional maturity and is usually thought of as taking place between the moment of birth and age eighteen
developmental disability	a handicap or disabling condition, such as autism, cerebral palsy, epilepsy, or mental retardation, that originates after birth but before the child reaches the age of eighteen and may be expected to continue
distractibility	responsiveness to extraneous stimuli; ability to be distracted
Down's syndrome	a condition caused by abnormal chromosome division and often characterized by a round skull, a flat nose, thick eyelids, and low mentality or mental retardation
dwarf	a person of short stature whose head and torso are of normal size but whose arms and legs are abnormally short
dyscalculia	impairment of the ability to calculate; inability to do simple arithmetic
dyslexia	impairment of the ability to read
emotional lability	rapid shifts in feelings, emotions, and moods
encephalitis	inflammation of the brain, usually as the result of infectious agents or their toxins
encoding	the act or process of expressing concepts, of putting thoughts into words
epilepsy	a condition in which some nerve cells in the brain become abnormally excited and the resulting unusual bursts of neural energy cause temporary loss of consciousness and uncontrollable spasms in affected parts of the body

Glossary
(continued)

epileptic	a person who suffers from epilepsy
etiology	all of the factors that cause a disease or abnormal condition; the history of such a condition
fetus	a developing human baby from three months after conception to birth
figure-ground	the relationship between what is visually focused on (the figure) and what surrounds it (the ground)
genes	the significant constituents of chromosomes by which parents pass hereditary characteristics on to their children
grammar	the study of the classes and types of words and their uses and relations in sentences; the rules governing the correct use of language
handedness	preference of one hand over the other
hydrocephaly	a condition of increased secretion of cerebrospinal fluid within the cranial cavity with a resulting buildup of pressure which may damage the brain
hyperactivity	behavior that is characterized by constant, random, erratic, and excessive motion
hypoactivity	behavior that is characterized by less-than-normal motion and can be described as lethargic
incoordination	physical awkwardness in activities such as running and skipping, writing and drawing
IQ	intelligence quotient; the score obtained when a person's mental age, measured by means of standardized psychological tests, is compared with that person's chronological age to yield an indicator of relative mental development
learning handicaps	disorders in one or more of the basic processes involved in understanding or in using spoken or written language, including disorders of attention, emotionality, memory, motor activity, perception, and symbolization
mental handicaps	disabilities that result in less-than-normal intellectual function
mental retardation	below average general intellectual functioning that originates during development and is associated with impairment in adaptive behavior
midget	a person of normal proportions who is unusually short
mislabel	to label or categorize incorrectly, often as the result of inadequate testing or hasty diagnosis
modality	an avenue of sensation, including audition, gustation, kinesthesia, olfaction, taction, and vision; the sense by which stimuli are received
perseveration	automatic and involuntary continuation of behavior
physical handicaps	disabilities that prevent or inhibit physical activity, including visual impairment, orthopedic handicaps, and disorders of body function
resource room	any instructional setting, other than the regular classroom, to which a child goes regularly for a specified period of time
rubella	a relatively mild and brief contagious disease characterized by red skin eruptions which may cause congenital defects in an unborn child if contracted by a woman during the first three months of her pregnancy
seizure	a sudden attack, as of epilepsy
self-concept	a person's idea of himself; the way a person perceives himself
special class	instructional setting designed to meet the unique or unusual educational needs of students who are handicapped or gifted to such an extent that these needs cannot be met in a regular classroom
Special Olympics	an international program of sports training and athletic competition for mentally retarded children and adults

Answer Key

Page 12, All People Have Feelings
Answers will vary.

Page 13, All People Have Talents and Handicaps
Answers will vary.

Page 14-17, Handicap Myth Game
Facts: 1A, 2B, 3A, 4A, 5B, 6A, 7B, 8A, 9B, 10B, 11A, 12B, 13A, 14B, 15B, 16B, 17B, 18A, 19A, 20B, 21B, 22B, 23B, 24B, 25A, 26A, 27B, 28A, 29B, 30B
Myths: 1B, 2A, 3B, 4B, 5A, 6B, 7A, 8B, 9A, 10A, 11B, 12A, 13B, 14A, 15A, 16A, 17A, 18B, 19B, 20A, 21A, 22A, 23A, 24A, 25B, 26B, 27A, 28B, 29A, 30A

Page 39, Beastly Braille
1. b = 1-2   2. a = 1   3. t = 2-3-4-5
4. bat = 1-2   1   2-3-4-5
5. bat =
6. guinea pig =
7. jellyfish =
8. Answers will vary.

Page 43-45, Getting Acquainted with Little People
Answers will vary.

Page 46-47, Accessibility Survey
Answers will vary.

Page 59, Fun with Words
Word meanings can be checked against glossary listings.

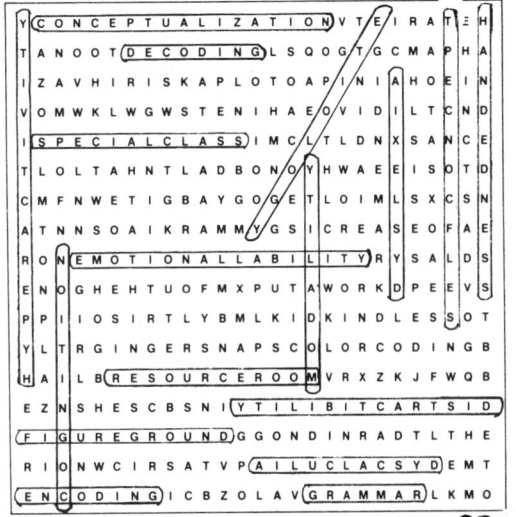

Page 60, Can You Follow Directions?
A correct paper should have no marks other than the student's name printed on the name line.

Page 61, Following Directions
The directions are as follows:
1. Print your name in capital letters in the upper right-hand corner of a piece of paper.
2. Underneath it, draw a circle that is 3 inches in diameter.
3. In the middle of the page, draw a square that measures 6 inches on each side.
4. When you have finished, raise your hand.

Page 63, Aren't You Finished Yet?

	a	b	c	d	e
1	0	3	9	6	9
2	49	79	48	58	128
3	7	93	24	105	109
4	66	11	83	20	96
5	86	63	25	68	90
6	54	110	65	12	46
7	48	21	46	122	121

Page 75, Fun with Words
Word meanings can be checked against glossary listings.

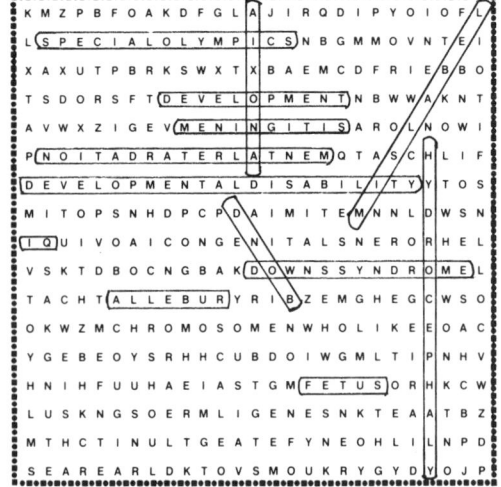

Answer Key
(continued)

Page 77-78, Tom's Story
1. seventeen years old
2. Anywhere, USA
3. no
4. It means that there are retarded people everywhere and that what happened to Tom could have happened anywhere in the United States.
5. yes
6. The text says that his name has been changed, but his story is real.
7. Tom has Down's syndrome, and he is mentally retarded.
8. A special school or hospital where people with special needs live and are cared for.
9. They decided to keep him at home.
10. Because they thought he would learn more and be happier.
11. Shake hands, walk, and other things they believed he could learn.
12. Answers will vary.
13. Answers will vary but should include ride the bus, go to school, hold a job, and make his own decisions.
14. He needs affection, recognition, and understanding.

Page 80, Smarties and Slowpokes, Sheet I
The instructions are as follows:

1. Draw a circle the size of a tennis ball on this page.
2. Draw a smaller circle on top of the first.
3. Draw a funny hat on top of the smaller circle.
4. Draw a face in the smaller circle.

Page 81, Smarties and Slowpokes, Sheet II
The instructions are as follows:

4. Write your teacher's name at the bottom of the page.
3. Write your room number above your teacher's name.
2. Put a circle around your room number.
1. Underline your teacher's name.